DUKE
STILL
SUCKS

Duke Still Sucks

*More Completely Unbiased Thoughts About
the Most Evil Team on Planet Earth*

By Andy Bagwell & Reed Tucker

Foreword by Tate Frazier

Art by Joel Tesch

Duke Still Sucks

More Completely Unbiased Thoughts About the Most Evil Team on Planet Earth

Printed in the United States of America.
First Printing, 2023
ISBN 979-8-218-12575-2

DukeStillSucks.com
Illustrations by Joel Tesch, joeltesch.com

To keeping hate alive. Even after a page turns.

Table of Contents

PREFACE

"I'm gonna write a book called 'UNC Sucks.'"

After we put out "Duke Sucks" way back in 2012, that was the No. 1 comment we heard. That book was a collection of essays examining why exactly so many people around the world felt the same way about the Blue Devils as they do about rhinovirus.

The idea grew out of a podcast we used to do called "Tar Heel Bred, Tar Heel Dead." If you hadn't guessed from that title, we, your humble authors, are UNC grads and bleed light blue. We used to end every podcast episode with that week's reason why Duke sucked, and never one time did we struggle for content.

So we started thinking about undertaking a larger investigation into Duke hatred, compiling an airtight indictment of that horrible little basketball team from Durham and its eternally insufferable (now former) coach. Turns out, the book had its fans, and it's still in print as we type this.

But it also had its critics. And that's where "I'm gonna write 'UNC Sucks'" comes in.

Weird thing is, years and years later, we're still waiting for that book.

The same goes for "Kentucky Sucks" or "Kansas Sucks" or "Villanova Sucks" or whatever other school you want to drop in there.

But we've got a sneaking suspicion that no matter how many times we check our local Barnes & Noble, those books are never going to appear. And the reason they're not is that there's just not enough material to fill them. A nice newspaper article? Maybe. A cutting tweet? Oh, no doubt. But a full-fledged book? Nah.

And the audience for those books might have trouble filling a decent-sized dorm room. UNC has its haters, but does that dislike rise to the level that would motivate readers to spend actual legal tender on an entire book? We seriously doubt it.

Duke is just different – and not in a good way. It has something special. Just seeing that D logo or those dark-blue uniforms evokes a hatred that is unique among the 350-plus teams that make up Division I basketball. The Blue Devils are what happens when God asks, "What would a professional wrestling heel look like as a college basketball team?"

And even though players come and go – sometimes within a matter of weeks – and even though legendary coaches move on, Duke is still Duke. The things we dislike about it don't change. They only evolve.

Occasionally over the years since "Duke Sucks" came out, we considered a sequel. Every single season seemed to bring new horrors. But finally, with Coach K retiring in 2022 and Duke and North Carolina meeting in the Final Four the same year, it seemed like the universe was telling us something. It was time.

What you hold in your hands is that sequel, covering all the Duke basketball lowlights since 2012. And once again, we didn't have to search too hard. The book practically wrote itself, and we fully expect to be back in a decade or so. See you then.

FOREWORD

by Tate Frazier

Hating Duke isn't a novel concept. It's been well-documented – not the least of which in the original "Duke Sucks" book – and by this point, everyone who's currently reading this second volume *gets it*.

I grew up in Henderson, North Carolina, surrounded by Tar Heels in my family. It was a given I would be indoctrinated into all things Carolina, especially basketball.

That meant I knew how to hate Duke before I even knew my ABCs. It's simple really. You know the tropes: It's public versus private, it's North Carolina natives against outsiders from the North, and, ultimately, it's Good versus Evil.

My parents drilled this into me from the day I was born at Maria Parham hospital back in 1993. We're a true Tobacco Road family. My mom graduated from UNC in 1982, and famously painted Chapel Hill Carolina blue after my pawpaw gave her a bucket of paint on the night Dean Smith won his first national title.

According to my parents, I was crying tears of joy in my crib as Donald Williams led the Tar Heels to Coach Smith's second national title over the Fab Five just a few weeks after I was born. Throughout my childhood, my older brother Gill and I rewatched a tape of that game countless times on our VHS player.

My parents dreamed we would both go to UNC, and fortunately we both did. I graduated in 2015 with a degree in broadcast journalism and ended up taking a job out in Los Angeles working with a sports guy by the name of Bill Simmons. Fast forward some 20 years later, and I chose Woody Durham's famous "technical foul, technical foul" call from the '93 title game to create the intro music for my podcast, "Titus & Tate."

It always comes back to Carolina basketball, and everything I know and believe can be traced back to being born a Tar Heel. It's a serious born-bred-dead situation. If you're a North Carolina native, college basketball is in our blood. That's why I feel incredibly fortunate to talk about the sport for a living. Most people are stuck with got-to jobs. I'm lucky enough to have a get-to job. I *get to* talk about college basketball – and not only that, but to talk about Carolina basketball, just like one of my idols, Stuart Scott, did on "SportsCenter" when I was growing up.

But this life has its downsides. It also means I have had to talk about the team eight miles down the road from Chapel Hill. And for many years, I had to talk about the man known by just one letter: K.

Until he retired, Coach K had been a constant through much of my life (except for the '95 season when he bailed and stuck Pete Gaudet with all those Ls), and he became the literal face of evil for me. When I watched "Star Wars," I'd picture K under Darth Vader's mask. When Voldemort was mentioned in the "Harry Potter" series I read as a kid, I'd picture Coach K's face. When the preacher mentioned the actual devil in church…you know where this is going.

Krzyzewski was the perfect adversary as a kid, and through him, I learned about good and evil in the world. My first lesson came when I heard the story of K calling out Dean Smith for a "double standard" when it came to treatment in the ACC. Now, Coach Smith is an untouchable figure in my home, so when I heard there was a coach who would say such hateful things about Smith, I was immediately done with him. The irony of it all is that K wanted that double standard for his own team.

With every Duke game I watched – witnessing the team's flopping and antics – my disdain only grew. I guess it was gamesmanship, but it represented the opposite of the Carolina Way. Then there was the fear K seemingly instilled in the refs and how that allowed his teams to stay in games and foul constantly without whistles blowing.

Things started to change around the time I went to college in 2011. All of a sudden, Duke was playing the one-and-done game, which was a complete contradiction to everything K supposedly represented. He went from the Wojos of the world to using USA Basketball to create a pipeline that funneled straight to Duke. He went from preaching a student-athlete approach to promoting the six-month stints of players like Kyrie Irving and Austin Rivers. And when five-stars like Semi Ojeleye or Joey Baker didn't work out, he'd kick them to the curb like Leonardo DiCaprio to a girlfriend who's old enough to legally rent a car.

Suddenly, it was like the world forgot who K was. People began to treat Duke like it was cool.

This is when I made it my mission to make sure the truth was not lost along the way. No matter what narrative K tried to spin, we knew the truth. We knew who he was deep down.

At the end of the day, it was and had always been about Coach K. Coach Smith would say that there's no I in team and emphasize things like pointing to the passer after an assist. Coach K would say that there may be no I in team, but there is a me in there, and he would point to himself for praise after Duke wins – and to Pete Gaudet after losses.

He's retired now, but during the 2021-22 season, which I dubbed "The Coach K Farewell Tour," he couldn't be avoided.

The hubris and hypocrisy on display that season raised some eyebrows, but to me, it was nothing new. That's who he had always been. And that's why what happened at the end of that final season was so poetic.

Being in the building in New Orleans with my family by my side felt like a fever dream, and the lasting image of K leaving the Caesars Superdome on the back of a golf cart will forever stick in my mind. No matter how much Duke tries to change the narrative, that moment in time will live on.

We'll all remember UNC's final two games against K, and you truly cannot spell Duke without K. You also can't spell wreckage. So as a Tar Heel and a fan of the game, it is with much joy that I turn it over to Andy and Reed to continue explaining why the Blue Devils do indeed *suck*.

Thanks for the memories, Coach K! We couldn't have asked for a more fitting finale!

"When Duke loses, America wins."
– New York Times best-selling author Nils Parker

DUKE
STILL
SUCKS

CHAPTER 1

COACH K RUNS TO THE ONE-AND-DONE

We may not have known it then, but 2010 marked the end of an era.

That April, the Blue Devils cut down the nets for their fourth national title, edging a surging Butler team by two points. Looking back, that Blue Devils team felt so incredibly Duke in a way that anyone who's only followed the team for a few years may have forgotten. They hustled, slapped the floor, and had a stable of goofy, annoying big white dudes like Brian Zoubek and Mason Plumlee who lived to do little more than set screens for scrawny shooting guards, like Kyle Singler, Nolan Smith, and Jon Scheyer.

It was the way Duke teams used to be built. That squad started three seniors and two juniors, valuing experience and a very particular personality type over world-beating talent.

The formula had a good run. It won loads of games for Mike Krzyzewski and caused opposing fans to scream obscenities and throw stuff at their TV screens for decades.

But then the next year, Coach K started to burn it all down.

College basketball had been changing and it wasn't hard to imagine that one day soon, it could pass Duke by. In 2006, the NBA raised the age of players who would be eligible for the draft from 18 to 19. Suddenly phenoms were no longer allowed to jump straight from high school, and they began hunting for a place to work on their jumper, get some national TV exposure and earn three sociology credits while they patiently waited for their birthday.

Ohio State made it all the way to the title game in 2007 by riding one-and-dones Greg Oden, Mike Conley, and Daequan Cook. John Calipari became the celebrated godfather of the genre, first at Memphis with talents like Derrick Rose, then later at Kentucky with (checks notes) every single player.

But Duke was Duke, and its program wasn't going to stop doing things their way, even if some of the fans were getting restless about recruiting.

"I would never recruit a kid who said, 'I'm just coming for a year.' I never have," Coach K said back in 2005. "For our school, we can't do that. A kid says, 'I'm going to come and use you for a year' — that's not what we should do."

K seemed to bristle at the idea that a player would turn down the opportunity to come play at a place like Duke – to get a distinguished faux-Ivy degree that you could then parlay into a job with a company owned by some wealthy booster, all while learning at the feet and getting cursed at by the greatest coach to ever do it. It was a privilege he was affording the players, not the other way around.

He'd said as much back in 1999 when Corey Maggette and William Avery bolted early for the NBA.

"None of those guys are bigger than the program," the coach said publicly. Privately, he was a bit more charming. "Your son is going to fuck my program," he told Avery's mother according to ESPN the Magazine.

The fans were also left grumbling. Duke's student newspaper, The Chronicle, likened the pain of Elton Brand and Avery's early departure to losing the 1999 title game to Connecticut. The basketball program, the newspaper wrote, should not bend to the changes in the sport.

"The men's basketball program must continue to focus its recruiting efforts on students who are keenly interested in completing their degrees," a column declared.

Cue the laugh track.

After the seventh-seeded West Virginia team upset Duke in the second round of the 2008 NCAA tourney, Coach K reportedly decided the program needed to evolve.

It started with Kyrie Irving. The celebrated New Jersey guard planned to study journalism, according to a report at the time, but everyone who'd seen him dribble a ball knew he wasn't going to stay in school long enough to learn even one of the five Ws. Duke recruited him anyway. In a not-so-subtle nod to the shifting power dynamic, Irving was allowed to wear No. 1 – the first Duke player ever afforded that privilege. Previous players had been denied because Duke was supposed to be No. 1.

From there, the trend snowballed. And it soon got absolutely gross. You could see Coach K selling out before your eyes in real-time, like when a celebrity is going through an expensive divorce and suddenly shows up in a commercial for reverse mortgages.

Austin Rivers stayed one year the following season, Jabari Parker came and went in 2013, Justise Winslow the next – the same year Jeff Capel claimed that Duke wasn't "going to be a team that's going to recruit a whole class of one-and-dones." By 2022, five players would leave early.

The new normal clearly wasn't sitting well with everyone in the university community. Some faculty, media and students took great glee in crapping on the early entrants. The Chronicle sports editor Chris Cusack penned an open letter to Irving in 2011, sarcastically urging him to go pro. "Don't follow in the footsteps of William Avery, you'll be warned; he made the wise decision to leave Duke after his sophomore year, and use the NBA as a stepping stone to an illustrious career in Europe," the student wrote.

Basically, everyone was picking up on the fact that this wasn't what Duke basketball was supposed to be. In 2018, a Duke professor suggested creating a continuing ed program to keep one-and-dones "engaged academically with the university in some way," in order to stave off the "reputational risk" to Duke. (As far as we can tell, only two one-and-dones in the sport have actually earned their degrees: UNC's Marvin Williams and Oden. If Zion Williamson ever steps foot in a classroom again, it will be as an exhibit in an anatomy class about how ankles are not meant to support an athlete that large.)

Duke was clearly becoming the new home of mercenary, purely transactional basketball – the thing Coach K swore he'd never do. But the gaslighting that went on in the intervening years was next-level.

The program, which had once taken great pains to make you believe it was about young men coming to get an education while they just happened to play basketball, now was going out of its way to craft a new image. The program was "all about the kids," and helping them could come in lots of different forms, including shuffling them off to the league in order to pay the six-figure jewelry debts they'd already racked up in college.

"If we get an outstanding player, and he does well and has the opportunity to go early, that's a business decision for him and his family. He has to do what's best for him," Krzyzewski told the Harvard Business Review in 2017. "But the question for any player should still be, 'How can that school make me better?' And ours still does, even in less time."

DJ Steward, Trevon Duval, and Avery might disagree.

But never mind how the players do once they leave Duke. The whole point of selling out was to win games – especially during March Madness. That was the ultimate arbiter. There was only one selection Sunday, one Final Four, and one champion. What's the point of winning signing day if it didn't translate into hardware and banners? Putting players into the NBA, especially if you get that splash of a first-round pick, is great for the brand, but if you aren't winning when it counts, isn't that an indictment that you might be doing less with more?

We recognize that this was a criticism of Dean Smith during the early years, but what K did during his one-and-done, soul-selling stretch was way beyond the NBA talent that came through Chapel Hill during the '70s, '80s, and '90s. Dean Smith had 25 NBA first-round picks in his entire 36-year career at UNC. Mike Krzyzewski had 25 in his last 11 years.

He loaded up on kids who had to pretend to go to school for a semester in an attempt to reel off multiple championships and cement his resume as the greatest college coach of all time. Instead, he left a messy record of bad defense, historic losses and a tournament resume that's softer than a one-and-done's GPA.

The question is, did the strategy make Duke a more successful team? Was getting these guys worth it?

Let's compare the Blue Devils to the other great one-and-done factory, Kentucky.

CHAMPIONSHIPS

Kentucky won it all in 2012. The top six players on that team had an average experience of 1.8 years and an average recruiting ranking of 13.8. They are definitely the highest-ranked and least experienced team to win during the 2011-2022 stretch.

Duke won in 2015. Their top six players had an average experience of 2.4 years and an average recruiting ranking of 17.8. This team relied heavily on senior guard Quinn Cook, so not entirely to the just-waiting-on-the-draft mold.

EDGE: A tie. But Kentucky won with the younger team.

FINAL FOURS

Kentucky: Three other Final Fours, including a loss to UConn in the 2014 national championship game.

Duke: Only one other Final Four, the historic loss to UNC in K's final game.

EDGE: Kentucky, plus salt in the wound for the ultimate rivalry loss.

BAD LOSSES*

Kentucky: One loss to No. 15 seed Saint Peters in the 2022 opening round. They also came up short in the round of 32 as a No. 4 seed to five seed Auburn in 2019.

Duke: Two bad losses against No. 15 seed Lehigh and No. 14 seed Mercer, both in the opening round. Ouch. They also lost as a No. 2 to seven seed South Carolina in 2017.

EDGE: Kentucky. Easily.

*We define a bad loss as an early-round exit or a loss to a double-digit seed.

MISSED TOURNAMENTS

Kentucky: Twice. Once in 2013, the year after they won it all and the entire team bolted for the pros. They missed again in 2021.

Duke: Once in 2021, the same year that Kentucky missed.

EDGE: Duke.

OVERALL EDGE

Kentucky. More Final Fours and fewer bad losses tell us that John Calipari knows how to one-and-done much better than K.

And not only did Duke underperform compared to Kentucky in the doing-more-with-freshmen game, the Blue Devils likely underperformed compared to where they might have been with a more diverse mix of players.

Judging by the teams that have won the NCAA title since the mid-2000s, it's pretty clear what the winning formula is. Fill a team with top-100 recruits, get them to stick around for three or four years, then supplement that veteran core with talented freshmen. Connecticut and Villanova won twice each with pretty much that exact formula. So did North Carolina in 2017 and Kansas in 2022.

Meanwhile, a 2019 Duke squad with three – three! – top-10 NBA draft picks got bounced in the Elite 8.

Betting on talent alone to take you to the promised land is like launching an Oscar campaign for The Rock. Sure, you may win, but honestly, the odds are not in your favor.

And what's more, if you put Coach K's one-and-done record up against the three decades before he sold out, loading up on the see-you-in-the-NBA guys made almost no difference to Duke's regular season records – and definitely hurt them in the tournament. So either K wasted a ton of talent during that time, or he was losing his coaching touch. We prefer to think it was both.

So why did he do it? What led to a seismic shift in team-building at Duke? Why run screaming from what seemed to be working?

Krzyzewski once told a faculty council that it was about staying competitive, and that in the end, athletes were responsible for their own choices.

We think there was more to it than that, though. It had to also be about ego.

Coach K was Duke basketball and if the program started to get left behind, so did its leader. And K wasn't going to stand for that. He and Duke had to be at the forefront of the conversation. Their game had to be the lead on "SportsCenter." They had to saturate magazine covers and draw continuous slobbering from every corner of the world. And if that meant changing in a way that made him a little uneasy, so be it. He became a crossing guard, waving a flashlight and directing players toward an on-ramp that led straight to the NBA.

And hey, the parade of big-name players he rented may have helped him rack up a few more regular-season victories, putting a more comfortable distance on the all-time wins list between him and his grumpy buddy Jim Boeheim.

And sure, championship banners were great and all, but in the end, it wasn't really about that. Duke was about winning the pre- and the regular season, on and off the court. Why have just one shining moment when you can have it all year long? Duke's loaded rosters had pundits and media drooling months before any of these "collegiate" athletes had even touched the ball. The preseason accolades fell on them nonstop, and ESPN spent the bulk of the regular season endlessly speculating about the draft status of the Blue Devils' starting five – even in games when Duke wasn't playing.

K got to stay relevant, and the players got valuable exposure that they hoped could boost them a few slots in the draft. The only rules: Don't overshadow the Dark Lord on your way out the door, make sure to add the #TheBrotherhood hashtag on your Insta and don't mention that tourney loss to Lehigh.

Kyrie Irving Is the Essential 21st-Century Duke Player

By Bryan Tucker

For decades, we had an idea of what a typical Duke player was. You know the type – a guy who made it on pure hustle. Someone you might even begrudgingly respect if you could get over the fact that he was loud, abrasive, whiny and had the same haircut as the bully in every '80s ski lodge movie.

Is that Duke player still playing today? Absolutely, but they're not the standard anymore. The past 20 years have changed what it means to be a typical Duke player. Coach K's one-and-done ethos has engulfed the Duke program like a dark fog. It has been transformed into a royal-blue G League for players on their way to greener pastures in the NBA. But all these players seem to have one thing in common: Their massive talent far exceeds their actual contributions to the game. Kyrie Irving is the essential 21st-century Duke player.

Kyrie is incredibly talented. You could make the case that he's the best one-on-one player in the NBA. But when you agree to put Kyrie on your team, you're not just getting talent, you're getting a Renaissance man. Kyrie wants you to know that he's much more than a basketball player. He's a thinker. And he really wants you to know this. His thoughts must be thrust into the public conversation so that all who doubt Kyrie's mind understand that he is more than just Uncle Drew. He's self-taught Professor Drew.

What Kyrie would most like you to know are his thoughts on the world. But not thoughts like Muhammad Ali had when he consciously objected to the Vietnam War. More like thoughts a kid in 10th grade has after he's just read Ayn Rand's "The Fountainhead" and now shows up to parties wearing a fedora. Kyrie's not saying the Earth is flat, he's just open to all possibilities. He's not saying that the Holocaust never happened, he just wants to "learn from all religions and possibilities." I'm not saying he's locker room poison, I just think it's an excellent topic for discussion.

Kyrie is a seven-time All-Star, and almost nobody wants to play with him. He's been on three teams so far and set fire to two of them. The third has been in danger of going up in flames for several years. Kyrie Irving's massive talent just isn't enough to overcome the inescapable fact that he is *a lot*. To win as a team with Kyrie means fighting against the tide of his swampy individual ego.

And this is where Duke comes in. How many Duke seasons in the past 20 years have started with enormous promise and ended in heartbreak? How many Duke teams have had the best recruits in the country, only to come up woefully short? Kyrie's 2010-11 Duke team had six NBA players on it. Six. Five of them are still playing in the NBA as of 2023. That team lost to Arizona in the Sweet 16. We all understand that Kyrie should win, but he just can't seem to get out of his own way. And his personal Duke experience has been repeated as a collective team experience in Durham over and over.

Have you ever heard Kyrie talk fondly about his days at Duke? Have you heard him tell anyone what valuable lessons he took away from his precious year in Durham, sitting at the knee of Coach K? He played 11 games there, and during that span he was featured in 500 ESPN promos. Kyrie as a college player was a trophy, a shiny object. His main value was that he was someone Duke could dangle to lure even more top recruits just like him. And those top recruits will stay for a year, garnering massive attention but few actual championships. And the cycle continues.

Tucker is a senior writer at "Saturday Night Live."

CHAPTER 2

THE ZION WILLIAMSON SCANDAL

The Duke basketball program has lots of superpowers – making Josh McRoberts seem like he was going to be a thing, for instance. But perhaps its greatest power has been its ability to convince the world that it is the university equivalent of Walter Cronkite – an honorable institution that holds itself to the highest ethical standards.

Can't you just hear Dickie V bellowing on an old telecast about how there's never been even a sniff of a scandal at Duke? "They come to the forefront of doing things the right way," the sportscaster wrote a few years ago.

Do they, though?

It doesn't take a Sherlock-level deductive genius to discover the Blue Devils have been hit by scandals and whispers of impropriety as much as – if not more than – most college programs out there.

That their rep remains squeaky-clean is a credit to the power of the media, the university, and the shoe company who all work on Duke's behalf to jam a particular narrative down our throats.

And nothing demonstrates that whole "nothing to see here" attitude better than the long, sordid case of Zion Williamson. His saga has enough pieces to build a respectable Netflix true-crime docuseries – wiretaps, fishy jobs, and shady bagmen hauling so much cash through the airport that they worried about getting stopped by security.

It all started back in 2018 when Williamson was among the top prospects coming out of high school. He drew arguably more scrutiny and press coverage than any prep player since LeBron James. Dude couldn't raise his hand in class without it making "SportsCenter Top 10." Two of his high school games were televised nationally on ESPN – which, if you're counting, is probably two more than the Sacramento Kings.

As the date of his college commitment drew closer, almost all of the experts agreed: He was going to Clemson. No ifs, ands or buts. He was from nearby Spartanburg, South Carolina, and the Tigers appeared to seasoned watchers as the clear favorite. The Crystal Ball projector at 247 Sports had Clemson at 87% to land the prized forward. The "hometown hero" narrative was seemingly etched in stone.

Clemson had definitely been putting in the work for months when it came to Zion. The school had even agreed to allow his brother, Tyriek, onto the track team as part of a package deal, according to Merl Code, a former Tigers point guard and Adidas rep.

On April 20, 2018 – the morning of Zion's announcement – word leaked to Clemson that he would indeed be choosing them. "Euphoria broke out in the hoops offices on campus," Code wrote in his book "Black Market: An Insider's Journey Into the High-Stake World of College Basketball."

But then something changed.

A few hours later during his televised press conference, Willamson reached under the table and pulled out – not a Tigers cap – but a Blue Devils one. He was going to Duke.

The press corps was stunned. CBS called his decision a "shocker." Even Duke had apparently been caught off guard, with one Cameron employee telling WRAL at the time that the school hadn't even drafted a statement to post in case Zion did end up picking Duke. The possibility wasn't even considered.

Kentucky and South Carolina had also reportedly been on Zion's short list. As had North Carolina. Legendary point guard Phil Ford had even agreed to pull his No. 12 jersey out of retirement for Williamson to wear. That kind of offer doesn't exactly come along every day.

Zion didn't take it. Instead, he curiously decided to join a Duke recruiting class that was already loaded with three other top-ten players – two of whom played the same damn position as Zion.

In explaining his surprise twist, Williamson said, "Coach K, he's just the most legendary coach to ever coach college basketball." Then he dropped the b word. "Like I said, the brotherhood represents family, and I'm all about family."

Well, family and maybe something else.

It didn't take long for the brotherhood narrative to get swept aside and an alternate one to emerge.

The first hint came in 2017 when the FBI announced it had arrested 10 coaches and Adidas reps on federal corruption charges. The Feds had spent months tapping the phones of several college basketball figures and had built a mountain of evidence that the whole system was dirty as hell.

The case initially had nothing to do with Duke. But when the trial went ahead a year later, the defense attorneys tried to introduce evidence of tapped phone calls involving another high-profile player – Zion.

On the intercepted call, Adidas rep Merl Code is chatting with Kansas assistant coach Kurtis Townsend about what it might take to land Zion.

"Hey," Townsend says. "Between me and you, you know, he asked about some stuff? You know?"

The "he" the men were apparently talking about, per the defense attorney, was Williamson's stepfather, Lee Anderson.

"I know what he's asking for," Code responded. "He's asking for opportunities from an occupational perspective, he's asking for cash in the pocket and he's asking for housing for him and his family."

So we know that Kansas at least was willing to arrange payment to Zion or his family. Other schools might have been, too. But Zion didn't choose those schools. He went with Duke – shocking everyone in the process.

The explanation could be completely innocent. Maybe he's a hardcore fan of dark blue. Maybe he really likes the brisket at Bullock's Bar-B-Cue. Or maybe Duke was willing to do something for him, too.

Coach K naturally tried to get in front of the scandal by sitting down for dozens of interviews and calmly explaining in great detail how all of this got misconstrued.

We're kidding. He batted the scandal away in typical churlish fashion.

"It's a blip," he said at the time. "It's not what's happening [in basketball recruiting]."

Maybe not, but something was definitely happening in Zion's housing.

After committing to Duke, he and his family moved to a 6,000-square-foot, five-bedroom house in a luxury Durham neighborhood – despite coming from modest means. Code claimed Zion's stepdad had once asked him for $100 because he couldn't afford groceries. Other schools are known to drop bags. Duke, like Glenda the Good Witch, was dropping houses.

Then came another blip.

Michael Avenatti – the high-profile attorney best known for repping porn star Stormy Daniels in her battle with Donald Trump – got embroiled in a 2019 slap fight with Nike. And during that ugly battle, Avenatti began leaking confidential information he supposedly had exposing college basketball's dark underbelly.

The lawyer fired off two tweets that likely induced more anxiety in Durham than Caleb Love. The first hinted that Duke was involved in something shady, and the second alleged corruption in Zion's recruitment. It specifically accused Nike of paying Zion's mother for "bogus 'consulting services' in 2016/17 as part of a Nike bribe to get Zion to go to Duke."

When asked about Avenatti at a press conference, a grumpy Coach K responded tersely, "There's nothing there," before walking out.

Then a few months later, Avenatti filed a court motion revealing alleged text messages among three Nike employees discussing money to be paid to Williamson and other coveted players while they were still in high school.

One Nike exec asked what the company was "willing to do ... whatever may be needed for the Zion…situation."

The recruiting coordinator responded that he'd be willing to do "35" for Zion.

Later, he added that they had "not presented our new offer" to Williamson and agreed that it was not a good idea "to put it in print" – always the hallmark of a legal, aboveboard transaction.

In the same batch of exposed text messages, another Nike exec admitted she was sweating bullets about the amount of cash she was being forced to sneak through airport security, and declared if she got stopped, she'd lie and say she had just sold her car. (True story: That exec, Rachel Baker, was hired in June 2022 as Duke basketball's general manager. Make of that what you will.)

Duke later claimed to have conducted a months-long investigation into Avenatti's allegations and turned up nothing. Though we're guessing their investigation was exhaustive in the same way the clerk at that one crap convenience store on the edge of town is exhaustive in checking IDs when teenagers buy beer.

Better luck next time, fellahs. One of these days we're sure you'll be lucky enough to connect the dots on an NCAA violation when almost all of the evidence is literally right there in a newspaper or court documents.

We should, of course, mention that Avenatti was later found guilty of trying to extort Nike and sent to prison. But just because he's crooked doesn't necessarily mean his information is wrong.

And we're more inclined to believe him because of yet another case involving Zion. The third blip.

It came a few months after Avenatti's allegations. Zion, who by that time had left Durham in order to gain an uncomfortable amount of weight with the New Orleans Pelicans, sued to be released from a contract with a sports agency called Prime Sports Marketing.

But his former agent, Gina Ford, wasn't having it. At all. She sued back, and in the process decided to spill all the alleged tea she had in court papers.

In one filing, she asked Zion to come clean about several issues, including that his mother and stepdad had "demanded and received gifts and economic benefits" not just from Nike but "persons acting on behalf of Duke University" to get Zion to become a Blue Devil.

Ford also claimed that Williamson or his family accepted "benefits from an NCAA-certified agent that are not expressly permitted by the NCAA legislation" while in high school.

She also dropped in a sworn affidavit that Zion's stepfather had accepted $400k from a Canadian marketing agent in October 2018.

And then there was the Durham McMansion Zion and his family were living in while he attended Duke. (It was a rental – just like his time with the Blue Devils.)

The court papers claimed the family moved from a house in South Carolina that rented for about $895 a month to the Durham house that went for around $5,000. The papers also alleged the house was owned by a Duke alumnus, and rumors at the time had it that the property was used as HGTV-style bait for recruits. "Come to Duke, where you'll get a great education – and an open-concept floor plan." (The News & Observer investigated the house's ownership and couldn't substantiate those claims.)

Ford ultimately lost her case against Zion. A judge voided the contract in 2021, ruling that Ford was not a certified agent in North Carolina.

Even so, the whole dirty business recalls the cases of former Duke players Chris Duhon and Carlos Boozer, whose parents also seemed to have moved up a tax bracket or two after their kids went to Duke.

After Duhon committed to the school in 1999, his mom landed a cushy job at a Durham money management firm owned by a Duke booster. Her position was apparently never advertised – according to newspaper accounts at the time – and when one employee questioned why the firm was hiring the woman, his supervisors told him, "Her son is going to play at Duke."

Boozer's family moved from Alaska to Durham in 2000 after the forward's freshman year.

Three months later, Boozer Sr. had a job at GlaxoSmithKline, a giant drug company run by a close friend of Coach K. When contacted by a reporter, Boozer Sr. at first said he worked as a computer programmer earning $125k. But after being told that his co-workers said he was an administrative assistant, he changed his story, saying he earned $40k.

Boozer left the job a few months after his son declared for the NBA draft.

Nothing to see there either, of course. Coach K once said that giving a job to a player's family member is "just a business decision," according to Ford's court filing.

And just to repeat: We have nothing necessarily against Zion or his family. Anyone who has children knows that they are bottomless money pits gobbling every last cent a parent can bring in. Thousands upon thousands of dollars dropped on plastic toys, velcro shoes, and Pokemon bullcrap. If we ever had a chance to turn the tables and earn a few bucks off our children, we'd be all about it. We get it. We're not mad about it.

It's Duke we have the problem with. Elite, untouchable, unsullied Duke.

Sham Duke. As Gina Ford's attorneys noted, Zion sure didn't seem eligible to play college ball. The dude was one giant, lumbering impermissible benefit for every single second of the two hours he spent as a Duke student. If nothing else, the school should be forced to vacate their wins that season and chalk up the losses to Pete Gaudet. (Look him up!)

And yeah, many of those rules Zion supposedly broke have changed since the advent of NIL, but they were the rules at the time, and schools and players were supposed to have been following them.

Still, if our decades of watching college basketball have taught us anything it's that it is in absolutely no one's interest to get to the bottom of the Zion situation. The NCAA wants to find out that Duke is crooked in the same way that a six-year-old wants to suss out what's really up with Santa Claus.

A scandal would have dinged one of the top brands in college basketball. And it would have tarnished the man who was being sold as the greatest coach in the sport and one of the faces of the NCAA tournament. It would have yanked back the curtain on college basketball and confirmed – completely, without a doubt, and once and for all – that corruption really is rampant. It's easy for the powers-that-be and even the fans to explain away misdeeds at UNLV or Memphis or Augusta University. We can all just tell ourselves those are isolated cases happening at fringe schools. They're outliers, don't-ya-know?

But when it happens at Duke, it becomes much harder to rationalize, and much more difficult to overlook. When it happens at Duke, you know the whole damn sport is rotten.

And that's probably why nothing ever sticks – and probably never will stick – at Duke. No matter how many wiretaps they show up on. No matter how many players are discovered to be buying hundreds of thousands worth of jewelry. No matter how many parents land curious no-show jobs.

Duke is Duke. And it has to remain Duke. For the sake of the university, the NCAA and the sport as a whole. To quote Coach K, these are business decisions. And business at Duke is good.

CHAPTER 3

DUKE'S WORST LOSSES SINCE 2012

March 16, 2012

Duke 70, Lehigh 75

The Stakes: First round of the NCAA Tournament. No. 2 seed Duke (27-7) versus No. 15 seed Lehigh (27-7)

The Team: The Lehigh Mountain Hawks had been to the tournament only four times prior to 2012 and had never won a game. The win against Duke remains their only victory in the tournament. In retrospect, this one shouldn't be too shocking if you ignore the seeding. Lehigh's star player, CJ McCollum, turned into a solid NBA player and had taken the team to the NCAA tournament as a freshman in 2010, losing to Kansas. This wasn't exactly a "happy to be there" situation. Earlier in the season, the Mountain Hawks had hung tough with a Michigan State team – led by Draymond Green – that was an eventual No. 1 seed.

The Play To Remember: Less than a minute to play. Lehigh is leading 65-59. The Mountain Hawks were struggling to inbound the ball after a time out when forward Gabe Knutson lost Duke reserve Michael Gbinije (who announced he would transfer from Duke exactly one month after this game) for a breakaway, uncontested dunk. Lehigh went up by eight with 47 seconds left, and the crowd and the players began to sense it. Lehigh might just pull this off. McCollum was the star of the team and the game, but our boy Gabe's only missed shot was a single free throw.

Why It Was Awesome: As the clock wound down, CJ McCollum walked over to the Lehigh bench and told his teammates to "act like they've been there before," leading to a somewhat muted postgame celebration. But there's no doubt this was an absolutely monumental victory. It had been more than a decade since a No. 15 seed beat a No. 2 seed, and it had only happened a total of 10 times in the history of the tournament. It still stands as Duke's worst tournament loss in terms of seed differential. Even the Dookies apparently couldn't believe it was happening. "At halftime, we were heading to the locker room, and I remember we heard Coach K going crazy through the walls, yelling at his team," forward Justin Maneri told Lehigh.edu. "They were clearly in shock. We knew we had something there. They were afraid." Earlier in the day, UNC had beaten Vermont in their first-round game in the same building, and nearly all of the Tar Heel fans hanging around were instantly converted to Lehigh fans. The atmosphere quickly started to feel like a home game for the Mountain Hawks. "You want to know what it felt like?" recalled fan Phil Cottros. "It felt like being there in the crowd in biblical times as David took down Goliath."

March 21, 2014

Duke 71, Mercer 78

The Stakes: First round of the NCAA Tournament. No. 3 seed Duke versus No. 14 seed Mercer.

The Team: The Mercer Bears from Macon, Georgia, had only made the tournament two times (1981 and 1985) before their matchup with Duke. Their team had five senior starters that had come close to making the tournament the previous two years. Their leading scorer was Langston Hall, whose name sounds like the place you had your 8 a.m. chemistry lab.

The Play To Remember: Or more like a series of plays. With 4:52 left in the game, Duke was up 63-58 and was poised to pull away. Mercer then went on a gritty 11-0 run, holding the Blue Devils without a point until 46 seconds left in the game. Rodney Hood turned it over. Rasheed Sulaimon missed a three. Jabari Parker missed. Hood fouled. Hood turned it over. Hood fouled. Andre Dawkins missed. And the game was basically sealed.

Why It Was Awesome: The game was played in Raleigh, North Carolina, at PNC Arena – close enough to Durham that plenty of Dookies made the trip and were sent home stunned and teary-eyed. Sweet. The shocking victory won Mercer the ESPY for Best Upset. Hard to argue with that. The win remains Mercer's only NCAA tournament win, and they hold a perfect 1-0 record against Duke. This was also the first year that K leaned hard into the one-and-done model and, this will shock you, but a team built around a five-star freshman looking to get to the League ASAP was horrid on defense. All year and all game against Mercer. The Bears sliced up the Devils on their way to shooting 56% for the game. Duke's team was led by the third-ranked player in the 2013 class, freshman Jabari Parker. The Bears were led by Daniel Coursey, the 277th-ranked power forward in the country and a one-star recruit coming out of high school. "Welcome to the club," Lehigh tweeted to Mercer after the game.

March 19, 2017

Duke 81, South Carolina 88

The Stakes: Second round of the NCAA Tournament. No. 2 seed Duke versus No. 7 seed South Carolina.

The Team: Gamecocks basketball can boast about winning back-to-back tournament titles. Never mind that they were NIT titles in 2005 and 2006. Coming into the weekend, they hadn't won an NCAA tournament game since the Nixon Administration but rode the victory over the Devils all the way to the Final Four.

The Play To Remember: South Carolina played horribly in the first half. There's no other way to describe it. And, somehow, they were only down seven at the half. After the break, they started off hot. When forward Chris Silva slammed home a breakaway dunk to cut the lead to one just four minutes into the second half, the crowd erupted. Duke suddenly got tight, and the Gamecocks went on to shoot 71% and score 65 points in the second half.

Why It Was Awesome: You have to understand, this Duke team was absolutely loaded. Historic. The Blue Devils were ranked No. 1 preseason. They returned a junior Grayson Allen, sophomore Luke Kennard and K's showcase one-and-done class of freshmen: Harry Giles, Jason Taytum, Marques Boldon and Frank Jackson, all of whom were ranked in the top 15 coming out of high school. And the Devils got bounced.

November 26, 2019

Duke 83, Stephen F. Austin 85

The Stakes: Actually, very little. Duke was No. 1 in the nation and was loaded up with another batch of five-star freshmen. Stephen F. Austin was queued up to be cannon fodder at Cameron for a late-November non-conference game.

The Team: Coming into the year, the Stephen F. Austin Lumberjacks didn't have high expectations, despite returning experienced players. They had gone 14-16 overall the previous season and finished ninth in the Southland Conference, which until right now you didn't know existed. They had also lost to Rutgers by 12 points six days before rolling into Durham. While this was historically their biggest win, they had pulled a few upsets in the NCAA Tournament, beating West Virginia in 2016 as a No. 14 seed and winning as a No. 12 seed in 2014.

The Play To Remember: There's no debating this one. The game was tight all the way through, ultimately going into overtime at 81-81. SFA scored first, then Duke's Vernon Carey Jr. responded. With six seconds left, Duke's Matthew Hurt fumbled a pass beneath his own basket and after a scrum, SFA's Gavin Kensmil picked it up. He tossed the ball to Nathan Bain who sped coast-to-coast, dropping the ball into the hoop as time expired. The Lumberjacks bench mobbed Bain. People all over the world celebrated.

Why It Was Awesome: There are few things better than sad Dookies in Cameron. One of those things that's better, though, is *shocked*, sad Dookies. Duke came into the game No. 1 in the nation and held a 150-game non-conference home winning streak. They hadn't lost at home to a team outside of the ACC in almost 20 years. 20 damn years! "I told our players, 'Banners can't beat us tonight,'" SFA coach Kyle Keller said after the game. "The players have to beat us."

An interview with Kevin Canevari

It was one of the most memorable sights in NCAA tourney history, a moment that launched a million gifs – and it didn't even take place during gameplay.

After the 14th-seeded Mercer Bears dispatched the third-seeded Blue Devils in rude fashion, pumped-up senior guard Kevin Canevari jumped into a circle of his jubilant teammates and busted out a passable version of the Nae Nae – a dance made famous by an Atlanta-based hip-hop group.

Canevari bent his knees, thrust out his hands, spun like MJ and slapped his chest.

The sheer joy of it was infectious, and Canevari – a reserve who averaged just a few minutes per game – soon became an unlikely star. The clip of his dance went viral, and in the years to follow, it would come to represent the unlikely upsets that make the NCAA so great.

We did some actual reporting and spoke to Canevari.

When you're sitting there during the game, are you planning this out? Are you telling yourself you're going to dance?
Definitely not. We had had fun dance circles after different games, like one time after we beat Ole Miss, but it definitely wasn't planned at all. It was in the moment and a rush of emotion, I just decided to dance.

Was your role on the team to be the celebration and dance guy?
Yeah. Most times I'm usually the one acting a fool. I will admit that. My teammates would say the same thing. I will crack jokes, dance, whatever it takes just to keep everyone as loose as possible.

Why the Nae Nae?
That was just the dance at the time, but you could probably tell that I hadn't practiced it a whole lot.

Did you have any idea that it would go as viral as it did?
I didn't think much of it. I definitely didn't know it would become what it became. We went back to the locker room after the game and someone came up to me, and they're like, "Hey, man, your dance is literally going viral. It's everywhere." By the time I got to my phone, it was just notification after notification, text after text after text. That's when I first started to realize, oh, wow, this is kind of crazy.

And then your team got nominated for an ESPY as Best Upset. What was that like?
Oh, man, it was one of the coolest things ever. We had just graduated college, 22 years old, and now we get to go to the ESPYs and be on the red carpet. We were living like rock stars. We were in the same boat as NFL players of the year and all these guys. We were at an event with our idols. It was just a surreal moment.

What's the craziest thing that has happened since that moment?

I would get recognized when I would go back to games at Mercer, but the craziest thing was when I got flown out to ESPN to be on the "Numbers Never Lie" show with Jemele Hill and Michael Smith. She had tweeted something about the dance, and some of my friends said I should tweet back to her that I could come on her show and teach her how to dance. Four days later, I'm on a flight to Bristol, Connecticut, doing the show.

You grew up in North Carolina. What teams were you a fan of?

I was more of a Carolina fan. I definitely was not a Duke fan. I liked Raymond Felton, Sean May, Ty Lawson and Tyler Hansbrough.

We'll buy you a beer for that dance alone the next time we see you.

Actually, I've got a quick story about that. Right after the game, we were leaving the locker room in full uniform and these five dudes decked out in Carolina gear came up to me and were like, "Dude, come to Franklin street. We got you. We are buying."

CHAPTER 4

THE WRONGEST HYPE SONG

It was June 3, 2021 – one of the most solemn and consequential days in Duke basketball history. The so-called greatest coach of all time was hanging up his whistle and deep lexicon of swear words after 41 years.

The press, K's family and a few fans and players had gathered inside Cameron for the occasion, waiting in hushed anticipation for Krzyzewski to bless them with an audience. Suddenly the lights dimmed and began flashing.

Then it happened: A wildly out-of-place Eurotrash soundtrack filled the cavernous arena.

Many in the crowd looked puzzled. Was this a press conference or a Dusseldorf rave? Was the athletic director about to hand out glow sticks and pacifiers? The few who knew what was up – or were still a little high off horse tranquilizers from the night before – stood and began clapping awkwardly along.

"I still hear your voice when you sleep next to me, I still feel your touch in my dreams," a processed female voice wailed over top of swirling synths.

Coach K appeared on one dimly lit side of the floor holding his wife's hand. She whispered something in his ear – our guess: "Skip to the next track!" – then K headed toward the podium at the front of the room just as the song kicked into high gear.

The sparse crowd began clapping more furiously – and out of rhythm– to the jackhammer beat, as K's wife urged them on.

"Cause every time we touch I get this feeling, and every time we kiss, I swear I could fly," the voice sang.

It was a bizarre atmosphere bordering on cult-like. You half expected the My Pillow guy to show up and start conducting a mass wedding.

The coach clapped along and half-heartedly pumped his arms for a couple of seconds as if to say, "I know this is absolutely terrible, but the kids like it, so whatayagonnado?" You could practically see his legacy leaking away with every terrible thump of the drum machine.

For many, the mash up of a high school dance and a press conference for a Hall of Famer was uncomfortable viewing. USA Today called the proceedings "awkward." One tweeter referred to the sight as a "fever dream."

But this was no dream, and anyone who's followed Duke basketball, attended a game at Cameron or owns a copy of "Now Das Is Vass Ich Kall Musik Vol. 14" probably recognized the song – "Everytime We Touch" by a German techno trio called Cascada.

The tune has been Duke's unofficial hype song since the 2000s when the school's pep band added it to the rotation. The then-new director Jeff Au wanted to introduce more current tunes into the mix, and the dance track – released in 2005 – fit the bill.

"At that time, it was played at all the parties on campus, and everywhere," band secretary Greg Caiola told The Chronicle in 2016. "It was that song you couldn't escape, and people seemed to get excited whenever the song came on."

The Crazies, for whatever reason, warmed to it – choreographing a dance that involved slow claps, fist pumping and probably muffled tears that this was their life now.

"Everytime We Touch" quickly became a tradition. It became Duke's thing. It was played at every home game, and Grayson Allen led a team dance at 2017's "Countdown to Craziness" preseason event, pogo-sticking across the floor like an evil Tigger. Cascada's singer, Natalie Horler, even appeared in a video leading the Duke class of 2020 in a virtual singalong.

"It's just weird," Au told The Chronicle. "You just never know which [song] is going to catch on."

You can say that again. The tune is among the most unlikely fight songs in history – mainly because it has nothing to do with, you know, the school or sports or basketball or competition or exerting yourself in any way beyond jamming an adrenaline injection into your dance buddy's heart after a ketamine overdose.

This is not a fight song. This is not a hype song. It's a would-already-be-forgotten dance song from Eurovision Song Contest castoffs that lifts its chorus from a lamer 1990s pop song and has no business being played in arenas.

Again, we are begging you to listen to the lyrics. Here's another taste: "Your arms are my castle, your heart is my sky. They wipe away tears that I cry." Sorry, are we preparing to play Wake Forest or journaling about one of the members of BTS?

Also, for a track that seemingly goes hard at 142 beats per minute, there's still something incredibly soft about it. Maybe it's the trashy synth sounds. Maybe it's the effervescent vibe. Whatever it is, the song doesn't get us pumped up as much as it makes us want to go write a cranky Medium essay about how music was better back when people played actual instruments.

And honestly, of all the weird stuff about Duke basketball – and there is lots – this is probably among the weirdest. Think about this for a second. Out of all the songs ever recorded, the university somehow settled on this one. Future NBA star after future NBA star has been forced to get their minds right for a big game while this bangs in the background. And the lasting memory many will have of the top name in coaching walking away is a blonde German lady harmonizing about a seemingly lost love. You could replay a simulation of reality a billion times over and never have that happen again.

But we wouldn't have it any other way, because "Everytime We Touch" is a gift to all Duke haters – a bottomless well of jokes. In fact, we're gonna challenge ourselves to write as many as we can right now. Ready? Start the clock, and let's go.

1. This song is so bad, it's the first thing a Duke Nike bagmen paid *not* to play.

2. The only thing more out of place at Cameron than this song would be a sophomore.

3. This song is so Eurotrash that the Duke cheer sheet just has a picture of Christoph Waltz.

4. This song is so Eurotrash that every Cameron Crazy now has dual citizenship.

5. This song is so bad, it explains why every Duke player only stays one year.

6. This song is so bubblegum, four out of five dentists recommend it.

7. This song's sound is more artificial than Coach K's hair color.

8. This song is such a poor hype song, it's responsible for the same number of Duke losses as Pete Gaudet.

9. This song is such a bad hype song, Coach K wanted to hang all his losses since 2005 on its record.

10. "Everytime We Touch" a Duke player while trying to play defense, it's called a foul.

    (OK, we're slowing down a bit here.)

11. The lyrics are more shallow than a brackish puddle that is dried up four days after a rainstorm.

    (Hmm. That last one wasn't so good. We might have to enlist friends to help out. Let's go to "SNL" senior writer Bryan Tucker.)

12. I wouldn't listen to this song if it was playing in my hearing aids.

(Solid.)

13. This was the first song at Borat's wedding reception.

14. This is what white people dance to when Taylor Swift is too ethnic.

15. This is the theme to every bachelorette party that's ruined your night out.

16. It's the official theme of 90s Mentos commercials – but in Europe.

17. This song makes ABBA sound like DMX.

    (Nice ones. Let's bring in our friend Martin Murphy. Go!)

18. This song is so bad it's played on a 24-hour loop during compulsory "Tae Bo Tuesdays" in hell.

    (We're not sure anyone knows what Tae Bo is anymore, but we'll take the joke. Let's go to David Drake.)

19. Cascada is so out of touch, my aunt won't even put it on her MySpace wall.

20. This track falls just behind "Silent Night" on the list of best hype songs.

Thanks for the help, everyone. See you at the club.

CHAPTER 5

ROSTER HIGHLIGHTS SINCE 2012

One consistent thing about Duke and the players that come through that Gothic hellhole is that the themes we zeroed in on in the original "Duke Sucks" book just continue to hold up. Need a complete douche that everyone hates? Check. Need a heralded big man whose career died after a short stint in Durham? Got that. Can we get a few useless, goofy white dudes on the team? Plumlee Shlumlee. We got more. What about a top-25 high schooler that gets immediately recruited over and transfers?

In "Duke Sucks," we covered 11 players. Here are 14 more since 2012. Meet the pre-transfer-portal all-stars.

Jalen Johnson, 2020-21

We can't decide if we love or loathe this guy. On the one hand, the top recruit quit on Duke in the middle of the season, announcing in February 2021 that he was foregoing the remaining games to ensure that he would be "100% healthy in preparation for the NBA draft." "But Jalen," you were probably screaming at the time, "What about your communications degree?!"

His move demonstrated an icky and unprecedented level of selfishness. We're not sure we want to live in a world where college athletes pull the ripcord as soon as their activities on behalf of a team represent the slightest personal risk. If everyone acted as crap as this, college basketball as we know it would be over.

Then again, you live by the one-and-done factory, you die by the one-and-done factory. Sooner or later, someone at Duke was going to do exactly what Johnson did. It was the only logical endgame when you recruit nothing but players whose biggest concern involves the outfit they'll be wearing on draft night.

And in the end, what really is the difference between a top NBA prospect who finishes a single season with Duke – often going out after an embarrassing early loss in the tourney – and Johnson? If you ask us, about 31 days.

Austin Rivers, 2011-12

Let's get this out of the way. Austin Rivers ruined what should have been a perfect day for us.

That day was February 8, 2012, and "Duke Sucks" had just come out the week prior. We spent the day doing radio interviews, walking around Chapel Hill and signing more books sitting outside The Pit on campus than we thought was humanly possible.

That night, No. 9 Duke was making that familiar eight-mile journey to Chapel Hill to take on No. 5 UNC. Like every game in that rivalry, nothing else mattered in the Triangle that day. WRAL opened its 6 o'clock newscast with a report, and when they cut to the reporter on Franklin Street, he was holding the book and talking about how it had just been released. Authors would kill their firstborn for that type of publicity.

We met a ton of amazing Tar Heel fans that day…just not many connected ones. Despite our best efforts, we couldn't secure tickets to the game that night. So we made our way to Franklin Street and plopped down in a bar to watch with the other lesser-thans who couldn't be in the Dean Dome. It was a tight game but with UNC up 10 late, we were sure we would be capping the night by rushing Franklin, reveling in the victory and likely getting second-degree burns in a bonfire.

But, no. You know what happened next. Every fan with even a passing interest in the rivalry knows what happened next.

Seconds left. Duke was down by two. Rivers got the ball. Pick. Switch. Rivers pulled up. Tyler Zeller's outstretched hand. Buzzer sounded. Swish. Duke won by one.

For that reason alone, we'll always loathe Rivers – but he does plenty to make others hate him, as well.

He seems to have an ego the size of the Target Center. In a 2018 interview with ESPN, for example, he weirdly claimed he had been the ACC Player of the Year during his brief layover in Durham. Nope. Tyler Zeller won it that year. Rivers didn't even get a single vote.

He's also a top-notch whiner – a trait he seems to share with lots of other players that come out of Duke. We'd be quick to say he learned that from Coach K, but on second thought, he might have picked it up from his father. When the younger Rivers played for his dad Doc Rivers on the Clippers in 2016, father and son were both ejected from the same game for complaining about the officiating. And then it happened again later in the season. Yes, really. They both got tossed two different times in the same season for whining.

In 2022, Rivers was ejected after picking up a double technical for appearing to throw an elbow at Lance Stephenson. He took to social media and complained about being mistreated afterward, but when you build a reputation like he has, you just ain't getting the benefit of the doubt.

Clippers forward Matt Barnes summed up his former teammate nicely. "Austin kind of rubs people the wrong way," he said on Mad Dog Sports Radio in 2018. "He talks a lot of trash and doesn't really back it up. I think people are probably tired of that."

We know we are.

Marvin Bagley III, 2017-18

Bagley was a freshman in high school when he helped his team, Corona Del Sol in Tempe, Arizona, win the state title in March 2015.

He joined Duke as the next heralded freshman one-and-done in September 2017.

Read that again. Those dates aren't typos.

We should also add that in that short window of time, he went to two different high schools and had to sit out one of those years because of the California Interscholastic Federation's rule that "a student may not be eligible to participate...if there is evidence the move was athletically motivated or the student enrolled in that school in whole or in part for athletic reasons."

But he wasn't just excelling on the court – he was apparently killing it in the classroom. Bagley decided to reclass after his junior year of high school, and during the summer of 2017, he somehow completed Algebra I, Algebra II, Latin and English just in the nick of time to pass admissions into Duke. Sure, and we've got a chapel in Durham to sell you.

Even notorious Duke homer Dick Vitale smelled a rat. "I'll give you another one that blows my mind: The academic geniuses, kids are juniors in June and all of a sudden in August, they graduate, reclassify," Vitale told ESPN. "I don't know what goes on behind the scenes — I'm not blaming any school involved — I think the high school, I think the people behind the scenes, wheel and deal. They become Rhodes scholars. It's a joke; it's a joke. The term student-athlete is a joke. We talk one-and-done; it's about time we do something about all of this."

The speed with which Einstein Bagley came to Duke a year early was not welcome news to the parents of the player who was supposed to be The Man that year at Duke – Wendell Carter Jr.

"My initial reaction, I was pissed," Carter's mother, Kylia Carter, told NBC Sports Chicago. "And it wasn't pissed because Marvin was coming. To be honest, I felt like that was information that was kept from us. It felt [shady], it felt like my baby was gonna get kicked to the curb. I felt like all of that."

"I felt like we were lied to," Carter's dad added.

As if the seemingly magical academic eligibility wasn't enough, Marvin's name also surfaced during the infamous FBI investigation of college basketball corruption. Yes, the same one that exposed the buckets of money thrown at Zion Williamson.

Tony Bland, then a USC assistant coach, was caught on video talking about how he was trying to get Bagley to the school. FBI informant Marty Blazer said on the stand during the trial that "Tony [Bland] needed money to get to Marvin. He wasn't going to go to UCLA or go to Duke," Blazer said of the discussion regarding Bagley's recruitment at that point. "Tony was confident he had Marvin Bagley locked in at USC."

And then he went to Duke. Anyone else sensing a pattern here?

It's hard to deny that Marvin had a really good season during his brief stop at Duke, and he went on to become the second pick in the NBA draft to the Sacramento Kings. Since then, he has had a decent, though injury-riddled, pro career but nothing close to the two players drafted after him: Luka Dončić and Trae Young.

Bagley was billed as the next Chris Bosh coming out of college. Turns out he might be more like the next Chris Dudley.

Jahlil Okafor, 2014-15

The hype around the center was deafening. Several outlets – including CBS Sports – named him the 2014-15 Preseason National Player of the Year before he'd even slapped the Cameron Indoor floor once.

The NCAA championship game that season should have clued us in that he was going to be another in the very, very long line of disappointing Duke big men. Okafor finished that contest posting just 10 points and three rebounds. Not exactly "I'm going to Disney World" numbers in what had been the most important game of his life.

No matter. Philly took him third in the 2015 draft and soon after, the wheels started to come off.

There were, of course, the injuries. Anyone can look at him and just know human legs weren't meant to support vigorous exercise on that body type.

Then there were the endless bad headlines. He got in trouble for fighting with Boston fans, for driving 108 in a 40 mph zone, for fighting in Boston again, as well as allegedly trying to use a fake ID at a Philly bar – despite being, you know, nearly seven damn feet tall and kind of famous around those parts.

His production in the NBA quickly tailed off, and his only reason for existence became trade bait. He got passed around more than a pipe in Chris Brown's private plane. He was shuffled off to the Nets, then the Pelicans before being foisted on Detroit. He went back to the Nets, was waived, then landed in Atlanta, where he survived on the roster for three weeks. In 2022, he headed east to play ball professionally in China. 再见!

Tyus Jones, 2014-15

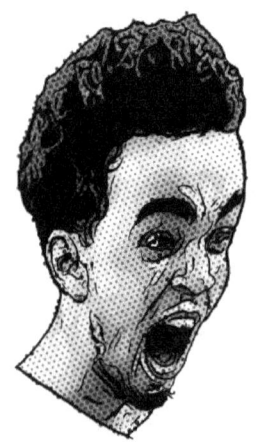

The point guard, like nearly every Duke player, only stayed one year at the school, but in his brief, shining time in the program, he became legendary for his mastery of the head snap – that annoying move where the dribbler throws his noggin back like he's being electrocuted at the slightest hint of contact to bait the ref into calling a foul. It's basically the guard equivalent of the big man flop. The move became so overused, the Blue Devils probably had to install a neck brace closet in the locker room.

It's a cheap move, and it started ruining college basketball so much that officials made it a point of emphasis a few years later. Call it the Jones Rule.

Mike Savarino, 2020-22

Finding out that Coach K's grandson was once on the team is actually less of a surprise than finding out Coach K has a grandson. Ascribing the human qualities required to be a grandparent to a man who once viciously cursed out teenage reporters is just very difficult for the human brain to compute.

Although Savarino is barely six feet tall and averaged just 7.3 points in high school, he somehow landed a scholarship spot on Duke's roster in 2020. The reasons why may be similar to how Sofia Coppola ended up starring in "The Godfather: Part III."

Grandboy's toughest challenge, aside from growing three inches, was trying real, real hard not to refer to Coach K as "Poppy " in public – as well as absorbing the skipper's salty language. "I know some people sitting behind the bench are just mortified by how many curse words he says, but he's a great man and he means a lot of good," Savarino once told The News & Observer.

The privileged legacy made the wrong kind of headlines in 2021 when he was arrested for a DWI, blowing a .08 on a breathalyzer. He sat out of basketball for a month and was later sentenced to 12 months of probation and 24 hours of community service.

In 2022, he took his 1.1 points per game average and transferred to Division III New York University. Here's hoping he started taking the subway home.

Harry Giles, 2016-17

We'd say he was the most head-scratching one-and-done in Duke history, except Cassius Stanley exists.

Although maybe that's not entirely fair to Stanley. He was far less hyped than Giles, who was built up to be the second coming of Hakeem Olajuwon and was once described by a Duke assistant as "the future of basketball." Seriously. We are not making that up.

But a string of injuries sidelined him through high school and then during his only season as a Blue Devil. He averaged just 3.9 points, 3.8 rebounds and only played 11.5 minutes per game. But if you thought those woeful numbers would have made him think twice about leaving the comfy confines of the Brotherhood – or make some NBA team hesitate to pick him – c'mon, man. This is Duke we're talking about.

Giles went 20th in the 2017 draft and ended up with the Kings. He bounced around among teams and the G League before suffering yet another severe injury in January 2022. Definitely a tough break for Giles, but he tried to stay positive. "Never Hate just wait on your turn," he tweeted in the summer of 2022. At this point, we're honestly kind of rooting for him.

Paolo Banchero, 2021-22

Please, please, Duke fans, tell us more about the Duke Brotherhood when Banchero and every other starter since the 2000s have been so out the door to the NBA that they sometimes put on a Cleveland Cavaliers jersey by accident on game day.

And few players better exemplified that mercenary attitude more than Banchero – a talented athlete who had an NBA-ready body even back in high school. In the Kevin Garnett days, he wouldn't have even paid lip service to going to Duke.

But probably the best thing about Banchero is how he so beautifully laid bare – yet again – the double standard that exists in this elite program of moral values.

Do you remember that Banchero was charged along with Savarino in that traffic stop for aiding and abetting a DWI?

And one quick aside to point out an amazing detail you might have missed on that whole situation: Savarino was busted driving Banchero's vehicle and Banchero was sitting in the back seat. Basically, Banchero was making Coach K's boozy grandson drive him around like it was an Uber. Make of that what you will.

Anyway, Banchero was charged, and if you thought the Duke basketball program would punish him for this egregious embarrassment and lapse of judgment – well, you probably didn't check how many points per game he was putting up.

Savarino was banished for a few weeks, while Banchero played. The. Very. Next. Contest. And started, no less.

When reporters questioned Coach K about how, you know, this seems kind of weird that one of your players can literally get charged with a legal infraction and receive basically no punishment, K retorted by calling Savarino and Banchero's cases "two different situations."

And of course, that's technically true in the same way that Lyle and Erik Menendez were two different situations.

"We're taking action," the coach claimed. "We took action and we will continue to take action...We had a violation of our standards, and we'll handle that internally. We've already handled – are handling it. But, violation of our standards. And that's it."

Paolo may have avoided time behind bars with that incident, but he apparently didn't totally escape that feeling while he was at Duke.

"Sometimes it'd feel like you was, like, a zoo animal or something, bro," Banchero said on the "Young Person Basketball Podcast with R.J. Hampton" in October 2022. "They would like, in class, you would see them over there whispering about you. Like, staring at you."

Probably wondering how to get a driver of their own.

Theo John, 2021-22

The big man transferred from Marquette in 2021 and only played for the Blue Devils for a single year, but he instantly bolted into the top 20 of most hated players.

Officially, he was listed as a "forward," but that title seems too expansive for what he actually did. He had one job, and one job only – to come off the bench, foul someone really hard and then chirp like he'd just won the NBA MVP.

In the 2022 game in Cameron against Carolina, for example, John eschewed the usual principles of defense and just decided to tackle Caleb Love. The Dookie was called for a flagrant foul. During the Final Four rematch between the teams a few weeks later, John was again in flailing mode, committing four hard fouls…in the first half. That's definitely efficiency, but maybe the wrong kind.

Even Duke fans apparently referred to him as "The Enforcer." "Look, this guy isn't particularly athletic and can't score or rebound," the fans seemed to be saying, "but when you need to lay the wood on an opposing player, he's your man." Good luck in the WWE, Theo.

Semi Ojeleye, 2013-15

Stop us if you've heard this one before. Heralded player comes to Duke only to molder on the bench for reasons no one can quite understand. It happened to Michael Gbinije – who left Duke to lead Syracuse to the Final Four. It happened to Chase Jeter, the No. 11-ranked prospect coming out of high school, who averaged just 10 minutes before bolting Duke and later selling his uniform on Instagram.

And it happened to Semi Ojeleye.

The 6-foot-seven forward – a former Kansas state champion – decided to leave Duke halfway through his sophomore year in 2014, having appeared in just six games that season. He and his family felt his getting buried on the bench was ruining his chances of ever playing professionally.

"He would have toiled away in obscurity," Semi's mother, Joy Ojeleye, told the Boston Herald in 2018. "He would have slaved away, and the dream would have been completely dead. Dead and forgotten. Another one who played in high school, went to college. Society would have just thought he never worked hard enough."

The family was especially upset because they said Coach K had assured them the year before that Semi would be playing.

Joy Ojeleye said she met with the head coach after Semi's first season – during which he played just 17 games and averaged 1.6 points.

"He said your son is an amazing person," Joy Ojeleye told the newspaper about her conversation with Krzyzewski. "'He's going to play. Don't worry. He'll be fine.' He even texted me and said Semi is going to do great, he's going to break out."

But the next year, when their son was again banished to obscurity on Duke's bench, the parents asked for another meeting with K.

This time, the family says the coach got enraged when asked about Semi's future and literally jumped out of his chair. Semi's terrified mom dropped to her knees.

"[Krzyzewski] shouted at me. He said, 'Am I lying, Am I lying?' Just like that," she said. "My oldest son said, 'Coach, she didn't say you were lying, she was only asking a question.'"

The mother had "tears streaming down her face." Two weeks later, her son announced he was transferring.

Semi's father, Dr. Ernest Ojeleye, said after the decision he got a call from then-assistant Nate James.

"He said the only way Semi was going to play at Duke was if someone else got hurt," Ernest Ojeleye told the Boston Herald. "Then he said Semi didn't work on his game, or do what they told him to do. He didn't ask the coaches what he had to do to get better."

"I said, 'No, this person you are talking about is not my child,'" the father replied. "I was really hot about this, but then I told him, 'Thanks for the privilege.' But it was really annoying for them to try and destroy my son's character. Very wicked, actually."

And not only wicked, but probably a little bit stupid too. Because Ojeleye soon moved on to SMU, playing for Larry Brown, and quickly proved himself a baller. During his final year, he averaged 18.9 points and 6.8 rebounds and was named the freakin' American Athletic Conference Player of the Year.

And, oh, yeah, then he was drafted by the Boston Celtics. Like, of the NBA. A professional team.

His career has been up and down since then, but he clearly deserved better than what he got at Duke.

Joey Baker, 2018-22

It's possible that in the entire annals of college basketball, no player has been done dirtier by a program than this poor bastard.

The five-star recruit initially committed to the 2019 Blue Devils class, but after some arm twisting, he enrolled early, with the plan to redshirt his first year.

Then came February 23, 2019, the 27th damned game of the season when – whoops – Coach K decided to burn Baker's redshirt against Syracuse.

K stuck out his gnarled, trollike finger, called Baker's number and inserted the forward into the game, shocking onlookers. Baker went on to play a grand total of five minutes. Five whole minutes.

Off the top of our heads, here are a few things that are longer than the amount of time Baker spent on the court leading to the loss of an entire year of eligibility:

The minimum recommended time to rest a steak after cooking.

"(Everything I Do) I Do It For You" by Bryan Adams.

The longest-recorded pee.

Baker should have been in high school taking a home ec test, instead, he found himself suddenly injected into a game at the Carrier Dome where his only purpose seemed to be to commit two intentional fouls at the half's end. He ended his five-minute stint with 0 points and a turnover.

Coach K later defended the curious decision to toss Baker's redshirt into the garbage and light it on fire, saying, "He's helped us because whether he gets on the court or not, he's helping us because he's in a different mindset, and he brings a different mindset to a practice and a competitiveness that helped us when we needed that."

What a crock of bullcrap.

Baker played just three more games and 13 more minutes that season and scored a grand total of three points.

It didn't get much better over the next few years. He never averaged more than 12 minutes in his Duke career, in part, because his head coach did his usual underhanded practice of recruiting over his current players. A parade of three-point specialists were brought in to gobble Baker's minutes like hungry, hungry hippos.

Baker stuck it out at Duke, for reasons that are probably only clear to his therapist. Now flash forward to his senior night, which unfortunately for him was also Krzyzewski's last game at Cameron. And you just knew that no one, but no one, was going to outshine His Highness that night.

Not only was Baker not recognized, he didn't even get into the game. Not even for a measly five minutes. He spent his final outing with a program he'd given four years of his life to riding the bench.

The lame explanation offered by Duke homers was that Baker wasn't honored because the COVID exception rule allowed him to return for one extra year, and the Blue Devils would, of course, acknowledge him at the end of the following season.

It never came.

The program announced Baker would be returning for that fifth year, but maybe they shoulda checked with him first. In the summer of 2022, Baker transferred to Michigan – four years too late.

Tre Jones, 2018-20

The dude was playing so deep in his brother's shadow that extra lights had to be brought into Cameron. But there's one thing older bro Tyus never had: his own classic #DukeSoDirty moment. During a game against Michigan State back in 2019, Tre Jones went up for a breakaway layup and landed on top of the fallen defender, Foster Loyer, jamming his foot into Loyer's chest in a way that would have made Christian Laettner smile, if Christian Laettner were a human being capable of smiling instead of a sentient hairstyle.

Jones did end the regular season on a high, winning 2020 ACC Player of the Year honors. But even that process had a little of that rigged Duke magic. Teammate Vernon Carey Jr. actually received 19 more All-ACC votes than Jones, but Jones took home the trophy because Duke nominated him and not Carey, taking the big man out of the running.

Kyrie Irving, 2010-11

Yes, we've covered him a little already, but we think he warrants more. He truly is a wonder, mainly for his mid-career shift from the face of Nike to that crazy uncle who rants at Thanksgiving dinner about chemtrails and subliminal advertising in cereal commercials.

He may have gotten the best Duke education 11 games could buy, but he still appears to have a few gaps in his knowledge base. Maybe the class that teaches you how to objectively evaluate reality was slated for his sophomore year.

The first clue came in February 2017 when Irving said some, er, questionable things about our planet – namely that it was flat. The star claimed that he believed this obviously insane thing because all the information about the planet's shape came from other people, and those people were lying to us.

Stop for a second and just marvel at the massive stupidity that is required to believe what Irving just said. Has he never been in an airplane and, like, looked out the window? Has he calculated how many people it would require to keep a conspiracy like that a secret? Has anyone he's known fallen off the end of the flat Earth? Maybe that's where Shelden Williams went.

But Irving wasn't finished. He also admitted that he wasn't sure the Earth revolved around the sun – an issue that was settled back when doctors treated sick people with leeches.

"For what I've known for as many years and what I've been taught is that the Earth is round," Irving explained. "But I mean, if you really think about it from a landscape of the way we travel, the way we move and the fact that can you really think of us rotating around the sun and all planets aligned, rotating in specific dates being perpendicular with what's going on with these planets and stuff like this –"

There's more to this quote, but honestly, we're gonna stop there cuz this dude is getting close to shirtless-bearded-man-in-the-New-York-subway-ranting territory.

Irving rightfully caught a ton of heat for his comments, and what he said actually went on to cause real-world problems. Science teachers reportedly had to reteach the curriculum to suddenly skeptical students. But then in an interview with The New York Times a few months later, the star player didn't exactly backtrack.

When asked if he believed the photos of Earth taken from space were real, Irving answered, "I do research on both sides. I'm not against anyone that thinks the Earth is round. I'm not against anyone that thinks it's flat. I just love hearing the debate."

Irving got wrapped up in another debate in 2021 when he was forced to sit out multiple games because he refused to get vaccinated for COVID-19. At the time, he started following and liking Instagram posts from a conspiracy nut who was claiming that "secret societies are implanting vaccines in a plot to connect Black people to a master computer for 'a plan of Satan,'" Rolling Stone reported.

Just a quick reminder here that U.S. News & World Report ranked Duke its ninth best university in 2022.

Irving was also partial to other wild conspiracy theories about aliens, one about how the U.S. federal reserve bank assassinated John

F. Kennedy and another about how the CIA murdered Bob Marley because the reggae singer "tried to bring people together and the fact that it was fundamentally built on love and truth, and we kill people for doing the right thing like that."

And we won't even get into his antisemitism controversy that ultimately led to Nike severing ties with him in December 2022.

There's likely no fixing Irving's views. When the star point guard left school back in 2011, he reportedly promised his father he'd get his degree within five years. In 2016, he pretty much abandoned that goal, apparently opting to get all the education he needed on 4chan message boards.

Rasheed Sulaimon, 2012-15

In 2015, Sulaimon earned the ignominious distinction of becoming the first player to get kicked off the team during Krzyzewski's tenure. And it happened in the middle of the season, no less, raising loads of eyebrows and questions across the basketball world.

Coach K at the time said that the junior guard had "repeatedly struggled to meet the necessary obligations." Then a month later, Duke's student newspaper dropped a blockbuster report that two female students had told peers that the player had sexually assaulted them during a retreat two years earlier.

(We're obviously not huge on Duke's basketball program, but the school's student journalism gets nothing but love.)

The paper reported that the head coach and members of the basketball program had learned about the allegations 10 months prior to Sulaimon's dismissal.

"Nothing happened after months and months of talking about [the sexual assault allegations]," an anonymous affiliate told The Chronicle. "The University administration knew."

"The Chronicle report ignited discussion of a possible institutional coverup," Sports Illustrated wrote in 2015. "This week on campus, 'What did Coach K know, and when?' emerged as a popular talking point."

It didn't help much that the Leader of Men refused to address numerous questions from reporters, citing privacy laws.

Sulaimon told ESPN in 2015 that the university questioned him about one of the allegations but that an investigation never progressed, and that, "I have never sexually assaulted, not only anyone on the Duke campus, but anyone period."

The two women did not pursue school or legal action because they feared the backlash from the basketball fan base, according to The Chronicle.

The whole case was about as ugly as it gets, from the allegations themselves to the sense that – yet again – a scandal at Duke basketball and the Hall of Fame coach gets treated differently.

If there is one small bit of amusing irony in this whole sordid mess, it's where Sulaimon chose to transfer after he was booted from the Blue Devils. He chose the school that Dookies probably hate most after UNC: Maryland.

CHAPTER 6

THE INCREDIBLE TRUE STORY BEHIND ESPN'S 30 FOR 30 'I HATE CHRISTIAN LAETTNER' – OR, WHY ANDY HAS TO OCCASIONALLY CALL THE COPS TO HIS HOUSE

The email arrived in the fall of 2014 and looked suspicious as hell.

"Would we be interested," the writer asked, "in being interviewed for a film about the Duke-UNC rivalry?" That was pretty much it. It was maddeningly vague.

You have to understand, when you're the face of Duke hatred, as "Duke Sucks" had made us, you get a lot of garbage emails. We made our addresses public, and because the barrier to sending an email is so low – it costs nothing, takes virtually no time and you don't even have to sign your name – the floodgates were open. Random people would write to yell at us, to call us names, to tell us, no, we were the ones who sucked. Others would claim we were just jealous. We'd have respected the haters more if they'd spent a few cents on a stamp.

So you'll understand our skepticism when this particular offer showed up. A film shoot, you say? Cut to us showing up at the set located in an abandoned Durham warehouse. Cut to a sack being pulled over our heads. Cut to a private jet flight to Mexico and a wood chipper.

But instead of ignoring the email, we wrote back. We'd been guests on plenty of radio shows and podcasts over the years. Sometimes these things work out. Our expectations remained low, however.

Over the next couple of weeks, we exchanged a few more emails with the producer. Where were we located, he asked. When could we film? Would both of us be willing to be interviewed, or just one?

We agreed Andy should be on camera. He's got an improv comedy background and is quick on his feet. He's also a borderline narcissist, and one of the most dangerous places you can be is between him and a camera.

All the while, the producer revealed almost nothing about the film. Was this guy a real producer, we wondered, or one of those producers in air quotes you always read that the movie business is apparently full of?

We kept pressing for answers.

Finally, the producer said he could tell us more but wasn't willing to disclose anything in writing. The details would have to come over the phone.

Andy took the call. The producer's voice was firm. He sounded sincere. They chatted about basketball and the "Duke Sucks" book. Maybe this was legit after all?

And then the producer dropped a bomb.

"This was not just a documentary about the Duke-UNC rivalry," he said. "It's a documentary about Christian Laettner."

Sorry, what? The Christian Laettner? He of the bad attitude, condescending sneer and The Game-Winning Shot Against Kentucky That Should Have Never Been a Game-Winning Shot? That Christian Laettner?

And then the producer said more – specifically the words "ESPN" and "30 for 30."

Time seemed to slow down and then stop altogether. Andy could feel the spit catching in his throat. For a moment, he forgot to breathe. Andy couldn't believe what he was hearing. This is one of the greatest series of all time. Each one is great. Have you seen the one about Michael Jordan in the minor leagues? We love this show and look forward to all the amazing stories that they tell every year. Some of the best filmmakers in the world making movies about sports? What could be better?

"But you cannot tell anyone about this right now," the producer said. "You have to be sworn to secrecy."

Andy was all in.

The plan was for the film crew to shoot a bunch of interviews in Chapel Hill that fall. Andy would meet up in a makeshift studio and spew some Laettner hate.

Flash forward to early October when Andy got a call telling him the studio wouldn't be available for filming. Would they be able to shoot at his house instead?

You know that anxiety you get when a boss or family member is coming over and you spend hours cleaning your house to a higher standard than what happens in a hospital before open-heart surgery?

Now imagine the cleaning that has to be done when your living space is going to be immortalized on film forever. It's insane. It's also not the recipe for a happy few days of marriage, by the way.

The day of the filming finally arrived. Andy's house was relatively clean. Or at least he shoved enough of his stuff into the garage to make it look presentable.

A van pulled up in front of his house and several large men started dragging big black cases up the driveway. The neighbors must have thought Andy was joining witness protection.

The crew walked through the door and the producer looked right past Andy. He stalked around the room like he was looking for a clue to a murder. Finally, he settled on a spot in the living room.

The hot lights clicked on and the interview began. Andy knew the game. The producers were no doubt looking for quippy sound bites, and Andy had prepared a few lines. The one comparing Duke to Cobra Kai made it into the final cut. The one about how a tiger never changes its stripes, or a devil never changes its horns, didn't.

The only question that came as a complete curveball was one about the rumors that Laettner and his Duke teammate Brian Davis had been a couple in college. The whispers had been fueled back in the early 1990s by a Sports Illustrated article in which Laettner proclaimed that only three things were important to him: basketball, school and Davis.

Andy hadn't prepared for that one, and he blurted out something like "I think he used that to his advantage." Then he scrambled to give the comment more context, worrying right up to the film's debut that he hadn't expressed himself very clearly.

The interview lasted a little less than an hour. The camera cut, the crew piled the gear back into the van and pulled away. And that was it.

Then the waiting began.

The documentary was scheduled to air in March 2015 – just in time for March Madness. Would anything Andy said make the final cut? If you know anything about documentaries, you know that they shoot way, way, waaay more footage than they'll actually need.

For a few months, Andy heard nothing.

In February he emailed the producer to ask if he was in the show. He'll never forget the reply that came back: "Oh, you're in there. A lot."

Uh oh. Was this a good thing? Andy tried frantically to remember exactly what he said during the interview many months before and what was going to get him sued.

The trailer hit in March. It was 30 seconds of pure hater glory. And alongside sound bites from basketball royalty such as Roy Williams and Jalen Rose, there was Andy's voice exclaiming, "I wanted to jump down and punch the dude in the face."

There was definitely no turning back now.

The film premiered in New York City on March 10. We got an email invite. And the invite mentioned that Laettner himself would be there.

Would he be angry? Had he even seen the film yet? Would he know who Andy was? Hating on someone through premium cable is easy. But in person? That was a different story.

Still, there was no way we weren't going.

We arrived at the building where the film was showing and rode the escalator to the pre-show reception.

"Let's find Laettner right away," Andy offered.

It wasn't hard. A seven-foot-tall head poked above the sea of people.

Screw it, we thought. We took a deep breath and approached him.

As we made our way across the room, Laettner locked eyes with Andy.

And that was the moment we knew – really knew – beyond a shadow of a doubt: He'd seen it. He'd seen the freakin' movie. Every single second of it. He knew exactly who Andy was and the horrible things he'd said about him.

We took a few more steps forward, snaking through the crowd and dodging waiters carrying trays of bar snacks. And when we looked up, there we were, standing just inches away from perhaps the greatest villain in the history of UNC basketball.

And that's the thing about villains. They rarely live up to their legend. They often seem ordinary. Standing face to face with them, it's hard to believe that they could be capable of such evil.

Laettner was wearing a tailored gray suit with a purple shirt underneath. And he was handsome in a bland, middle-aged sort of way. If he had been a foot shorter, you might have mistaken him for a concierge at a business-class hotel. He was still thin and athletic, but his age was betrayed by a few lines on his face and graying hair. The cloud of arrogance you expected to follow him around like seagulls chasing a trash barge just wasn't there.

He seemed…normal. Human, even.

"Hey, Christian," Andy said. "I'm not sure if you know who I am, but can we get a picture?"

"Oh, I know who you are," Laettner replied with an unexpected flatness in his voice.

We snapped a picture together and filed into the theater. This was going to be fun.

The lights went down and the film rolled. Just a few minutes in, Andy appeared on the screen. And then appeared again. And again. We weren't sure how many sound bites the director would use, but Andy ended up with nearly as much screen time as Laettner.

We don't need to tell you that the film is a masterpiece. It's a fun watch that captures an important piece of the UNC-Duke rivalry and an important character within it. But it's also a smart exploration of hate and tribalism in sports, as well as a meditation on whether villains can be redeemed.

As the credits rolled, it dawned on Andy that his life was about to get much more interesting.

The film was followed by a Q&A. Laettner mentioned that he almost went to play at Carolina, and he suggested that he and Andy might have been friends. (Let's not get ahead of ourselves.) The two would have lived on the same hall though – true story.

Laettner's old teammate Grant Hill was also there and lectured Andy and the other haters about how Laettner had actually been a great NBA player and insisted we didn't know the real Christian.

Maybe. You can accuse Laettner of lots of things. Of being a bully. Of running a shady real estate business. Of amassing huge debts that nearly landed him in the slammer. But being a bad sport – at least in his middle age – probably isn't one of them. He sat there that night through the whole film and the questions afterward, absorbing all the crap Andy, WWE personality Peter Rosenberg and others had to hurl at him. And he did it with, dare we say, a touch of humility. (Or maybe he was just trying to prove he had the temperament to get a coaching job. We'll probably never know.)

The rest of the night is a blur, but as we filed out of the auditorium, we're 99% sure we caught Laettner's nine-year-old son throwing Andy a death stare.

The show aired on ESPN a few nights later. The angry tweets started arriving even before the first commercial break. It seemed like every Duke backer on the planet took to Twitter. In the same way that Laettner gave physical form to the abstract concept of Duke hatred – a convenient vessel into which UNC fans could throw all their vitriol – Andy now served that purpose for Duke fans.

"You should have called your film '30 for 30 Butt Hurt from an old bitter man,'" wrote one hater.

"Andy Bagwell is actually making me forget why I hated Laettner and reminding me why I can't stand UNC-CH," piled on another.

Andy got called "stupid," "a loser" and a "douchebag."

But that night was what Twitter was made for, and when the insults continued to flood in, Andy's kids thought it was the greatest thing ever.

He also got a lot of love from UNC fans, as well as Kentucky supporters. The critics also approved. Mostly.

NPR called Andy a "professional Duke hater." High praise. USA Today noted that Andy summed up the film's premise by stating, "No one's going to ever top Laettner because people don't stay in school long enough now."

Variety did call him "overused." Like Laettner, we can't win them all.

Over the next few years, the fame from that documentary appearance followed Andy. He got recognized often, and in the weirdest places.

He was at Home Depot one day, and this random woman and her kid walked up. "I hate Christian Laettner too," she said before walking away.

Later in the year, Andy was out Christmas shopping and stopped for a drink. The film happened to be playing on one of the TV's ringing the bar.

Andy knew what was coming next.

After Andy's face had popped on screen for a second time, the guy sitting next to him turned, mouth agape, and asked, "Is that you?" He bought Andy a beer.

The film still airs occasionally on ESPN and when it does, the Twitter mentions blow up all over again.

But there is a downside. Andy has had to call the cops to his house – and not just once.

One time when he was out of a town in Kansas City, his wife called him freaked out because someone had left multiple threatening messages on their answering machine. "You need to go to a hospital right now and die," the obviously drunk man growled.

The police showed up quickly and instead of being alarmed, they thought it was pretty funny that in sleepy Cary, North Carolina, someone was getting death threats because of a TV appearance.

The cops ultimately tracked down the caller. Turned out he lived in Charlotte. They knew what kind of car he drove and everything. In the end, Andy decided since the guy wasn't local, the threat of a drive-by was minimal, and the cops went on their merry way.

But not all random phone calls required police intervention. Andy has gotten at least one message from an anonymous UNC fan expressing admiration. (Thanks, my guy, but next time just send an email or slide into the DMs.)

The film has also kept the original "Duke Sucks" book on the shelves far longer than the publishers ever thought was possible, and for that, we are grateful.

And what about Laettner himself? Does he still think of the documentary and about that one talking head in it who was courageous enough to call out his "floppy hair?"

A few years back, one of Andy's friends took his son to a Laettner basketball camp. During a quiet moment, the dad decided to have a word with No. 32.

"Hey, I'm friends with Andy Bagwell," the dad said. "Do you have anything you want me to tell him?"

"Who?" Christian answered, confused.

"The 'Duke Sucks' guy," the dad answered.

A flicker of recognition passed across Laettner's face. "Oh, that guy," he said dismissively. "I'm trying my best to forget about him."

Delicious. Still living in his head.

Hate Sampler

Enjoy a small, small selection of the messages sent Andy's way after the 30 for 30 premiere.

Logan Kadolph @LoganKadolph · Mar 30, 2022

@ncbags sounds like a junior high girl that doesn't get her way on the Christian Laettner 30-30. So annoying!!

Bart Woodcock @woodcockba75 · Mar 22, 2015

@ncbags just watched 30 for 30. And realized you are such a cry baby. Laettner didn't even mean to cut monstross. You are such biased unc

K.L. Culver @Kalebc25 · Mar 25, 2015

@ncbags you should have called your film "30 for 30 Butt Hurt from an old bitter man". Your probably a patriots fan, that would be amazing.

K.L. Culver @Kalebc25 · Mar 25, 2015

@ncbags how about "I hate when old men can't grow up and act mature"? Good title? I will work on it

K.L. Culver @Kalebc25 · Mar 25, 2015

@ncbags how much did miami pay suh? He has stepped on two players, never suspended or thrown out of the game.

K.L. Culver @Kalebc25 · Mar 25, 2015

@ncbags you come off as a sniveling 45+ yr old douche in your documentary. Teams get screwed over all the time. Grow up. Jesus christ.

Tim Ryan @TheSportsHernia · Mar 23, 2015

Finally saw the @30for30 on Laettner. Had completely forgotten how much he expertly antagonized players and fans. Also, @ncbags needs meds.

⎁⎁⎁   💬 2   ⟲   ♡ 1   ↑

nkellyPHFan
@WhoIsNark

Also @ncbags is a ferret cunt who's mad he didn't get into Duke so he wrote a book about it. That is all

2:16 AM · May 4, 2018

CHAPTER 7

THE UNIVERSITY STILL SUCKS

When someone says, "Duke sucks," you probably think of the basketball team. They are, after all, the centerpiece of Duke suckitude. But Jon Scheyer and his merry band of floor slappers are hardly the only things that stink in Durham.

There's also the university itself. And in our previous book, we dug into the school's origins, its founder, its architecture and on and on. Our conclusion: We're not fans.

Yeah, OK, from an academic perspective, Duke can hold its own. A $13-billion endowment and an estimated cost of attendance damn near $90k per year will buy you a lot of teaching talent and beakers for the science lab.

But we couldn't help notice that from a cultural perspective, there's still a certain suckitude that permeates through the entire university and most anyone associated with it.

We've rounded up some of our favorite news stories since 2012.

Duke University: Trademark Bullies

Duke has produced more than its fair share of bullies on the basketball court over the years. Matt Christensen, Theo John and the list goes on. So when we stumbled onto the story that Duke was far and away the biggest trademark bully amongst U.S. colleges, we were intrigued.

How did they qualify for such an honor? Who discovered this? What is the best way for us to make fun of them for something that we don't fully understand?

For answers, we look to none other than two Duke University law students, James Boyle and Jennifer Jenkins.

Back in 2020, they published a research paper called "Mark of the Devil: The University as Brand Bully" detailing, with a wealth of data, that Duke goes way over the top in opposing any trademark submissions that might possibly be confused with the university.

And just to clarify, Duke is not at or near the top of the bully list compared to other universities. They're near the top among all companies doing business in the United States. Think of that for a second.

The gist is this: People are submitting trademark requests all the time to the United States Patent and Trademark Office. Other people or institutions can oppose those submissions if they feel the submission infringes on their own trademark or name.

That makes sense. We get that. Protecting brands and intellectual property is important. In some cases, we wish that protection was more aggressive. It might have saved us from that time we ended up buying a bar of "Dave" moisturizing soap from a New York dollar store.

Duke, however, goes nuts with the opposition. Just about anything with the words "Duke," "blue" or "devil," an image of a devil and the letter "D" itself (we aren't kidding) is flagged and opposed or challenged. Here are just a few real examples:

"Pretty Devil" slot machines - OPPOSED

"Blue Ball Chiller" alcoholic beverages - OPPOSED

"Get Your Blue On!" for a charitable fundraiser - OPPOSED

"Geek'd" for clothing items - OPPOSED

"Beach'd" for beach bags and cosmetic bags - OPPOSED

"D'Grill" for barbecue smokers and grills - OPPOSED

Boyle and Jenkins looked at three different categories of schools – top academic institutions, top athletic programs by revenue and reputation, and top basketball schools. Each and every time, Duke came out as the biggest offender, and it wasn't even close. The school files far more oppositions than most of the schools in the top 10 combined, and 85% of those filings are just as completely absurd as the examples we just gave.

It's fascinating. And, unfortunately, it works. Many times, just the mere filing of an opposition makes people give up and move on to something else, no matter how frivolous the claim is.

What the paper doesn't address though, is why? Why is Duke so protective? We think we know the answer. It fits right in with the deep paranoia and sense of entitlement that drives so much of its behavior. It's the same reason they own the dukesucks.com address and the same reason they apparently made that ownership private after we called them out in our last book.

At the risk of running afoul of their trademark, there's a word for people who engage in this kind of behavior: D'bags.

Tallman Trask – Murderer of Light Rail

Charlie Reece @CMCREECEARCHIVE · Feb 27, 2019

6/ Duke's decision to kill the light rail project **sadly** reinforces the worst fears of many Durham residents — that Duke University is an arrogant and elitist enclave with little interest in being the kind of partner this city needs.

/end

22 81 196

For nearly 20 years, the governments of Durham and Orange counties worked together to plan a light rail transit system to help alleviate the Triangle's choking traffic. Voters approved a sales tax hike to fund the project in 2011, which was already two decades in the making. That was so long ago, that Coach K's hair was still black – sorry, never mind.

By 2019, the project came to a head. Planning had already consumed $130 million of public money, and with construction set to start the following year, another funding deadline loomed.

And then Duke University killed it deader than Pete Gaudet's career.

It was a complicated project that still had a few hurdles to overcome, but at the end of the day, Duke slapped down a veto card. The school refused to cooperate with the project or join a mediation to iron out its issues, which the school had had several chances over the years to express.

Their official reason had something to do with the train line disrupting the medical center, but this was NIMBYism at its finest. Duke vice president Tallman Trask III (who has quite possibly the most Duke name ever) was the university's point person on the project and eventually let the clock run out on any last-minute compromises.

As Durham City Councilman Charlie Reece so perfectly tweeted, "Duke's decision to kill the light rail project sadly reinforces the worst fears of many Durham residents — that Duke University is an arrogant and elitist enclave with little interest in being the kind of partner this city needs."

NC Policy Watch editor Billy Ball added on Facebook. "A reminder that Durham, perhaps the only place left on Earth that didn't hate Duke, now hates Duke."

Duke Still Thinks It's An Ivy League School

Duke has always tried to convince the world that it is no different from the true Ivy League. As we wrote in the last book, they built their campus to look like Princeton, even fake-aging the chapel's steps to make the building look older than it really was.

But Princeton's not the only Ivy they've stolen from. In 2022, they moved on to Harvard.

That's when Duke student Priya Parkash delivered a commencement speech that bore a striking resemblance to one delivered by Harvard's Sarah Abushaar eight years before.

Analysis by Harvard's newspaper and others found several passages that appeared to be lifted wholesale. Both speakers waxed on about their feet collecting "a world of experiences," both joked about going through airport security as non-whites and compared their campuses to independent countries.

Harvard's Abushaar joked that her school's version of the Statue of Liberty was a John Harvard statue, while Duke's Parkash joked that her school's version of Christ the Redeemer was the statue of James

Buchanan Duke. Puh-lease. The enormous sculpture of the Christian icon outside Rio de Janeiro is considered one of the New Seven Wonders of the World. The statue of our boy James is an old white dude holding a stogie who built the university with dirty tobacco money. If you're going to plagiarize, at least go with something that doesn't make us roll our eyes into the backs of our heads.

We shouldn't be surprised by the controversy though, as it's just yet another example of Duke trying to be something that it's not. The Brotherhood. The Gothic architecture. The Harvard-like speech. Peel back a single layer and it's all a lie.

And there's one footnote that makes this story even more Duke. According to Chapelboro.com, no one involved in the scandal was punished in the immediate aftermath – not Parkash for what seemed like an obvious honor code violation, not the official in the president's office responsible for vetting the speakers. Parkash did apologize though. Sort of. She blamed her friends for feeding her the stolen material via a statement written for her by a pricey crisis PR firm.

Larry Moneta Does Not Like Rap Music. Or China.

Joe Van Gogh is a coffee shop on the Duke campus. Larry Moneta was Duke's vice president for student affairs. And while Moneta appreciated a cup of hot tea and a vegan muffin, there's one thing he apparently did not enjoy: rap music.

In May of 2018, Larry made his way into Joe Van Gogh, as he often did. A young woman named Britni Brown was working the register that day and was responsible for the store's playlist. At the moment Moneta walked in, Young Dolph's "Get Paid" came on. We will admit, an unedited version of the song is probably not the best thing to play in the middle of the day in a coffee shop, but Brown said she was unaware it was on the playlist. Honest mistake it seems. Larry, however, couldn't let it be.

As another barista, Kevin Simmons, made his tea, Larry admonished the staff – who, by the way, immediately apologized. Larry paid for his order and huffed out.

That really should have been that. He was a regular at the place and nothing like this had ever happened before. The employees changed the song when he complained.

But as Larry angrily sipped his tea and nibbled on his dairy-free mini-cake, he probably thought, "What would K do?" The Leader of Men would certainly not have it end there. Larry made a phone call.

On the following Monday, Brown and Simmons were called into Moneta's office. Except he didn't have the cojones to show up. A human resources person, Amanda Wiley, took his place instead. According to an audio tape of that meeting acquired by The INDY, she said, "Duke University has instructed us to terminate the employees that were working that day." Larry later denied that he told anyone to fire Brown and Simmons, trying to have his vegan muffin and eat it too, we guess.

About seven months after that incident, Larry took a trip to China to check in on Duke's campus in Kunshan and decided to post some wackiness on Facebook. "Reasons to move to China … NOT!" he wrote next to photos of "Mexican Tomato Chicken Flavor" potato chips, an air quality report and a toilet.

Never mind that he was using "NOT" – the stalest comedy punchline this side of "I can't even." His posts also seemed a little…how to say this? We'll let Michelle Li, president of Duke's Asian Students Association, take it from here. "It's obvious to us from the posts that they are, at best, very culturally insensitive and, at worst, very racist," she told The Chronicle.

We can't even with this guy.

Larry took a "hiatus" from Facebook after the incident, before taking a more permanent break in 2019. He retired from Duke.

Tallman Trask and the Adventures of Parking a Silver Porsche

We should have known that Tallman Trask III wouldn't have stood for a mode of transportation that forced him to share space with commoners.

Long before he was killing off the Durham train line, he was tooling around in a silver Porsche we'd like to imagine had "The CompensatingMobile" painted on the side.

The car literally ran into trouble in 2014. While Trask was hurriedly trying to park his car to make the Duke-Elon football game, he was stopped by parking attendant Shelvia Underwood as she was directing a pedestrian. As she turned back to the car, Trask hit her, knocking her to the ground, according to a court complaint.

Underwood alleged – and witnesses corroborated her story – that Trask called her a "stupid [N-word]" as he drove off.

TT3, as we now call him, initially denied hitting Underwood. That is until The Chronicle presented him with a photocopy of a handwritten apology note he gave to Shelvia after she filed a complaint with the university. (Student journalists again!) Both parties lawyered up, and suits were filed. Of course, TT3 never copped to using the slur, but this whole thing just reeks of the privilege felt by some of those in the Duke orbit. They are convinced they're above it all and will deny, deny, deny until they can't anymore. Better repair any damage to that hood of your precious vehicle, T. You definitely won't be able to catch a light train from whatever hole you crawl out of every morning.

CHAPTER 8

THE SEMESTERHOOD

Back in October 2015, Duke's then-assistant coach Jeff Capel tweeted congratulations to Quinn Cook, who was attempting to make the Cleveland Cavaliers roster. (The former Blue Devils guard was cut a few days later.)

The tweet was little more than a snooze-worthy platitude. "So proud of this guy," it read in part. "A fighter and champion" – the social media equivalent of one of those motivational posters you might see in an office supply store.

But the message was anything but innocuous. It was just 16 words long, but that simple tweet has left a terrible legacy that we are all still living with. Because at the message's end, Capel decided to tack on a few filler hashtags.

And with that, Duke's wretched Brotherhood was born. Or as Capel wrote it, #thebrotherhood.

Duke's massive marketing machine, in conjunction with Nike, quickly seized on the term. The machine sputtered and smoked and roared to life. Suddenly, #TheBrotherhood branding was everywhere.

The message was simple: Playing for the Blue Devils bound you to every current and former person who had worn the uniform. You were now lifelong best friends, part of a special unbreakable network who would support each other until death or rival shoe contracts do you part, amen. And at the center of this magical brotherhood, the glue that bound it all, was Coach K – the man who had taught these young men more about basketball, life, and cursing than anyone thought possible.

The message's blitzkrieg-like rollout was so powerful and sustained, you'd be forgiven for being gaslit into thinking this #Brotherhood business had always been a thing at Duke. It must have been carved into one of the cornerstones at Duke Chapel, they had you thinking. How could you have been a basketball fan for years and never heard of this concept? Had you just missed it?

You hadn't. It was nothing more than a crass marketing gimmick, no different from "Coke is it!" or "The quicker picker-upper."

And to understand why, you have to appreciate what was going on with Duke basketball at the time and the power of propaganda.

Years ago, fine young men came to Duke, stayed four years, played a little basketball, and got a great education and a degree along the way. But as we've covered, that all changed when Coach K sold his soul to convert his program to a one-and-done clearinghouse.

By the middle of the 2010s, Duke's program was increasingly populated by players who were using the national platform Duke offered as little more than a springboard into the NBA. Guys like Kyrie Irving, Jabari Parker, Justise Winslow, and Jahlil Okafor were bolting before they'd even finished unpacking their Playstations in their dorm rooms.

That flew in the face of Duke's image as an elite learning institution, as well as a place where players had the rare opportunity to learn at the feet of The Greatest Coach Ever (™). It also didn't sit right with some Duke fans, many of whom were no doubt grumbling about the newfangled way of doing things.

Many of these fans had gone to school there, and they had a snobbish attitude about all things Duke. How, they questioned, could those players not appreciate all those opportunities they were being given? "This is not how they did it in my day," they muttered.

The one-and-dones made Duke's basketball program – and the school, by association – look mercenary, like it was sinking to the level of those other unsavory institutions, such as Kentucky, that Blue Devils fans had taken great glee in criticizing over the years.

It seemed their precious Duke University was becoming just like those other schools.

And this is where the propaganda comes in. If you've spent even a single second following politics or world events, you know that an often effective way to counter negative publicity is to just say the opposite. You may not be able to change the bad things that are actually happening but you can sure change the narrative around them.

When cigarettes started to get criticized for causing health problems in the mid-20th century, tobacco companies suddenly rolled out lots of ads featuring doctors proclaiming stuff like, "Luckies are less irritating."

And when Duke's program looked less prestigious in some eyes, the marketing machine desperately needed a counterpunch.

And they found it in #TheBrotherhood. Phony or not, the concept was perfect because it struck back at the exact thing that was making some Duke fans – and if we're being honest, some basketball fans in general – uneasy. It reassured fans that, yeah, none of this is like it used to be, but we're still offering these basketball players something valuable, something Duke-centric that we can all take pride in. It promised doubters that even though it doesn't look like these players have loyalty to the university that you love, they actually do.

Nonetheless, the narrative still had one problem. It was a tough sell. It felt eye-rollingly inauthentic.

But a lack of truth is hardly a dealbreaker. It's a problem lots of marketers face, and there's a reasonably easy end-around. All the messenger has to do is blast out the counter-narrative, repeating it over and over again until the audience gets so ground down or confused they give up.

In advertising, they call it ad nauseam. Whatever you call it, one thing is clear though: It works.

Since at least the 1970s, studies have shown that hammering a particular message over and over and over again makes an audience more likely to accept it as true and to stop questioning the motivation behind it.

And as luck would have it, one way to increase your chances of success is to have your message driven by a snappy, memorable slogan…like #TheBrotherhood, for example.

And that's just what Duke did. Suddenly #TheBrotherhood was everywhere.

Duke unveiled special uniforms bearing the slogan. Their marketing department ginned up a nearly five-minute hype video called "The Brotherhood" featuring dozens of current and former players. The slogan began appearing all over the basketball program's social media accounts.

By the time high schooler Zion Williamson held his 2018 press conference to announce his commitment, the term had entered the college basketball lexicon. The marketing push was working.

"I will be joining the brotherhood of Duke University," Williamson said in his strangely worded acceptance.

Marvin Bagley said something similar before coming to Duke in 2017. "The brotherhood there, that's what Coach K preached to me and my family," Bagley said during his own announcement.

The question that you're no doubt asking is, how much brotherhood – sorry, #Brotherhood – can there possibly be among players who stay in school barely long enough to earn a single sociology credit? These guys hadn't even spent enough time on campus to know where the dining hall was, much less to develop deep, lifelong friendships.

Kyrie Irving played just 11 games for the Blue Devils – but he once hawked a line of pricey "Brotherhood" Nike sneakers.

Jalen Johnson, a five-star recruit, quit the team in 2021, just 13 games into his freshman year.

This isn't a brotherhood, it's a semesterhood.

And then there are the transfers. Even before the NCAA transfer rules changed in 2021, Duke saw an alarmingly high number of players bolting Durham for greener, less Coach K-filled pastures.

Alex O'Connell and Joey Baker appeared in that Brotherhood hype video intoning, "We will play together," and, "We will give Duke our best." Both soon chose to give other teams their best. They transferred.

But that's OK. They'll always have #TheBrotherhood, remember?

"We aren't here forever," Jayson Tatum, who left after his freshman year, reminded us in the same hype video. Talk about understatements.

To be clear, we've got nothing against the players. We think every college athlete – and that certainly includes Duke's basketball players – should be free to pursue the opportunities that come their way. And if some NBA team is willing to pay them enough money to install an ATM in their living room – as the Dallas Mavs' DeShawn Stevenson did – they should take it.

What's galling is the disingenuous slant Duke's spinmeisters are putting on the program. True brotherhood is built through years of shared experiences and bonding through adversity, not four months of sweating in the same colored jersey.

And there's one more thing that rubs us the wrong way about #TheBrotherhood. Duke stole it. From North Carolina.

Don't believe us? Listen to Roy Williams.

"Yeah, they stole it but they're intelligent, they gave it a new name," the former UNC head coach said at a 2018 press conference.

One other thing you have to remember about Duke: The school seems to have an inferiority complex about its lack of history. It desperately wants to be old, and venerable and have traditions stretching back hundreds of years. It so wants to be the Ivy League.

But it isn't.

The modern-day version of Duke dates to just 1924. That's really old if you're talking about, say, milk. But when it comes to institutions of higher learning, it's younger by a couple of hundred years than America's oldest.

Duke's patron, James Duke, badly wanted a Princeton – founded in 1746 – and he had Duke built in the Gothic, looks-older-than-it-is style of the Ivy Leaguer.

The school's basketball heritage is similarly limited.

You could argue that Duke basketball didn't really become a national brand until Coach K arrived – and maybe not even until the program's first national championship in 1991.

That's several decades of history, but it's not even close to the long traditions built at Kentucky or UCLA or Kansas, where the guy who freakin' invented basketball coached.

And, of course, it doesn't hold a candle to North Carolina.

By the time Coach K punched in at Duke in 1980, Dean Smith had already been the head man at North Carolina for nearly two decades. He was already a legend, and he had built his vaunted Carolina Family.

And he built it organically. We repeat, organically. No one with a marketing spreadsheet decided the Carolina Family should be a thing. It simply flowed out of the values and the goodness of the man who led the program.

It was one of the things that set UNC apart in the basketball landscape.

And Duke didn't have it. So they borrowed it. Shamelessly.

Capel didn't exactly deny the charge when asked about #TheBrotherhood during a 2018 appearance on 99.9 FM The Fan.

"Look, we all copy from each other. Because one place has 'family,' does that mean I can't call my family 'my family?'" he asked.

No one's saying you shouldn't. But when it comes to marketing pushes used to brand a program, lure recruits and sell merch, it's best to just be straightforward. Why not leverage a program's reality instead of creating a fake one? Just be honest.

Maybe it's time to shelve #TheBrotherhood and go with $TheLivelihood instead.

CHAPTER 9

COACH K'S KRAP KOACHING TREE

In the original volume of "Duke Sucks," we examined Duke's coaching tree, and honestly, the whole exercise left us wanting. That thing was less a mighty oak and more of "A Charlie Brown Christmas" tree. Wilted. Sad. Dropping needles everywhere.

With Coach K's cursing off into the sunset in 2022, we were once again deluged by articles about what a strong family of coaches The Dark One had seeded into the NCAA and NBA ecosystem.

Coach K may be gone, these articles insisted, but don't worry. Just like your pepaw who passed away in that nursing home, he's still with us. But instead of being a creepy ghost who haunts your attic smoking Hav-a-Tampa Jewels and demanding Werther's Originals, Coach K lives on through his legacy of coaches that have studied at his loafered foot.

Really though? Can you name a single coach off the top of your head that came out of the Duke system?

"Alexa, set a timer for 10 seconds."

Time's up. Did you come up with anything? Maybe Mike Brey. Maybe. And we'll give you that one. He's done a respectable job at Notre Dame of putting the roundball on the map at a school where football comes first and every other sport comes a distant 34th. He has even managed to make the tourney most years.

But beyond Mike Brey, the quality drops off faster than the "Star Wars" franchise.

Let's revisit the Duke and Coach K Koaching tree.

Jon Scheyer

He's not only the successor to Coach K, but he's also the subject of one of the saddest Google autocomplete searches of all time: "Did Jon Scheyer play in the NBA?"

Look deep into your heart. We think you already know the answer.

No matter his credentials, or lack thereof – he'd never been a head coach before he took over the Blue Devils' bench – he's doomed to fail, right? There's absolutely no way K's hubris would allow him to pick someone who actually might show him up.

As a Duke player, Scheyer was less known for his play than for what some called "Scheyer Face" – his habit of contorting his mug every time he touched or shot the ball like he was birthing a hippopotamus.

As a coach? Who knows. Check back in a decade or two, when that Google autocomplete will have probably morphed to, "Where is Jon Scheyer now?"

Chris Collins

At one point, we were absolutely certain he was going to take over for Coach K at Duke. Collins had it all: an elite pedigree by a quirk of birth, a snotty attitude and a hustling white guy on-court persona. But instead of ascending to the top of Mount Hair Dye, he got passed over for Scheyer.

It might have been because Collins' record at Northwestern was nothing to write home about. Sure, he had one magical year back in 2017 when he took the Wildcats to their first-ever NCAA tournament. But he quickly followed up that milestone by posting losing records in the next several seasons, including going 8-22 in 2019-20.

It's pretty clear by now: Collins is never going to be his dad. His heart's just not in it.

Nate James

James took over at Austin Peay in 2021 and burst out of the gate by immediately posting a losing record in the Ohio Valley Conference and overall.

He's just the latest character in the same old story: Schools hire a former Duke assistant in hopes of getting Coach K – only one that's cheaper and hopefully more pleasant.

James himself didn't dispel this narrative that he would be like a Coach K klone – a vessel for all the knowledge the former leader of men vomited into him.

"It's just an endless amount of knowledge that's consistently poured into you each and every day, each and every season," he told USA Today about his years working for K. "You try to soak up and drink up as much as you possibly can."

Keep drinking, Nate.

Steve Wojciechowski

Wojo – the original floor-slapping, vein-popping, short white dude – was supposed to be a home run when he was hired at Marquette in 2014. But then, the usual story unfolded. Cue the underachieving. Cue the dashed expectations. Cue the failure to live up to the Coach K name.

It's hard to convey just how much Wojo bombed at Marquette, a once-solid Big Ten program that had gone deeeeep into the NCAA tournament in the three years before Wojo's arrival. His winning percentage was historically bad for Marquette. Only Georgetown more regularly underperformed against preseason expectations during his stint. He failed to win a single tourney game.

He was so disliked by the Golden Eagles supporters that a #firewojo hashtag got trending. The fans got their wish in the spring of 2021.

Quin Snyder

Is it just us or does this guy look like his soul is being kept in a magically sealed box buried in a dark cemetery while his physical body must survive horrific things like sunlight and interpersonal interactions?

He creeps us out for some reason. So does his record. This guy has bounced around the basketball ranks more than a journeyman center with a bum knee.

He quit at Missouri back in 2006 after becoming the target of alleged recruiting violations and posting a ho-hum record. Then he joined the NBA ranks, first in the D-League, then with the big boys. His stint as the head man in Utah ended in June 2022 after eight seasons – probably due to his pathetic postseason record with a team that often had respectable talent.

Tommy Amaker

No matter how many W's or L's he piles up, he will still be remembered as the man who presided over a cheating scandal at Harvard.

Harvard, y'all. Harvard!

After being cut loose by Michigan – and being paid a reported $900,000 to walk away – Amaker took over the Ivy Leaguer in 2007. A year later, The New York Times published a shocking article alleging certain, er, improprieties in recruiting. The resulting investigation led to the first NCAA penalties ever slapped on the basketball program.

Even Jerry Tarkanian – the coach known for one of the dirtiest programs ever to grace college ball – had a laugh at Amaker's expense.

"Harvard?" the former UNLV coach told Yahoo! back in 2008. "Harvard's cheating?"

The school would be rocked by yet another scandal in 2012. More than 100 students – including Amaker's top two players – were accused of cheating on an exam in a course called "Government 1310: Introduction to Congress." Insert your own lame joke there.

The players later left the school. Amaker remained to continue shepherding the program into mediocrity.

Mike Dement

We covered him in the previous volume, and he's seemingly retired. But we just wanted to point out that after the former Duke assistant resigned in 2011 from the head coaching job at UNC Greensboro, he was replaced by none other than Wes Miller. The former Tar Heel took a program that Dement had run into the ground and turned it around completely, winning four conference titles and making two NCAA tourney appearances in ten years. Once again, a Tar Heel upstaged a Dookie.

Johnny Dawkins

Hey, look. It's another Dookie given the keys to a high-profile program, only to fizzle out after a few years.

In this case, it was Dawkins and Stanford. He was let go in 2016 after eight seasons – and only one NCAA tourney trip for a team that used to be a near-annual presence during Mike Montgomery's tenure. On the plus side, Dawkins and the Cardinal did win the NIT in 2012 and 2015, which does earn you banners…we think?

Instead of going away quietly, Dawkins sued Stanford for millions. Great idea, Johnny. It's not like Stanford has any high-profile attorneys floating around on the alumni roster to smack that out of court.

He then moved on to the head job at Central Florida where his son, Aubrey, transferred from Michigan to join him. He won at least 18 games four times during his first six seasons with the Knights, and it did seem like Johnny had found the perfect spot to coach in a mediocre way in a mediocre conference at a school more focused on its football program. Things officially get tougher with UCF stepping up to the Big 12 in 2023, and we expect Johnny to get replaced with a coach who can actually coach. Our advice to UCF: lawyer up now. There's a history with this dude.

Bobby Hurley

Hurley's coaching career started hot out of the gates. After three years as an assistant under his younger brother Danny, he took over the head coaching duties of the Buffalo Bulls in 2013. They had gone 14-20 the previous year and finished fourth in the MAC Eastern Division. In his first season, the Bulls finished 19-9 and won the regular-season conference title. They then lost to Eastern Michigan in the first game of the conference tournament, eight days before Hurley's alma mater fell to Mercer in the first round of the NCAA tournament. You hate to see it.

The next year, Buffalo again won the regular season, this time taking the conference tournament crown and advancing to the NCAA tournament. They were ousted in the first round by West Virginia.

What happened next? Bobby bolted. Arizona State came calling and decided to cast their fate with one of the whiniest players of all time, and the results have been … predictable. ASU has hovered right around the .500 mark with a few highs (ranking No. 3 in the country in 2017-2018) and a few lows (losing to Syracuse in a First Four game in that very same season). After being ranked 18th preseason going into 2020-2021, ASU finished 11-14 and followed that up with a pitiful 14-17 in 2021-22.

The one through line, however (and this is going to shock you), is his constant complaining, run-ins with the refs and a heaping helping of technical fouls and ejections. Here's a brief history of his lack of control:

First year with Buffalo (2013-14) – He got hit with seven technical fouls over the season.

Second season with Buffalo – Hurley had four technical fouls, including one that came just 55 seconds into a game against Toledo.

January 4, 2016 – In his first conference game as ASU head coach, Hurley flipped out after a call went against his team against Arizona and was promptly ejected. Way to get off to the right start with the PAC-12 refs there, Bob.

January 28, 2018 – The PAC-12 publicly reprimanded Hurley for criticizing the refs after an overtime loss to Colorado.

February 25, 2018 – The PAC-12 again reprimanded him, and this time threw in a $10,000 fine for good measure after he chased a referee off the court following a loss to Oregon State.

March 3, 2018 – Hurley got smacked with a technical toward the end of a game against Stanford for yelling at the refs, and it pretty much cost ASU the game. They lost by one. This was also right around the time school president Michael Crow told azcentral sports that Hurley needed to "learn how to manage his volcanic emotions."

January 30, 2021 – This one was actually pretty funny. After a no-call in a game against Stanford, Hurley jumped up and stomped his feet on the ground, before hurling abuse at the ref. He promptly lost his balance and fell on his butt. Before he could start laughing at himself, the ref popped him with a technical, quickly snapping him back into Ballistic Bobby mode. Your reputation has preceded you, whiny one.

January 23, 2022 – After yet another postgame freak-out following a loss to Stanford (what is it about The Cardinal that makes Hurley go crazy?) in which two ASU players got involed, the PAC-12 suspended Hurley and guard Jay Heath for one game. Hurley was also fined $20,000, while player Jalen Graham was reprimanded.

"The actions of the head coach and student-athletes were in clear violation of the Conference's standards of conduct, and will not be tolerated," Pac-12 commissioner George Kliavkoff said in a release.

It's not just that Hurley has a fiery personality and has a knack for racking up technicals and ejections. He clearly has no problem with his players getting into the act, as well, and simply cannot learn from or chooses not to care about past mistakes. Bobby's coaching career is seemingly hurtling towards one of two ends: He flames out and gets fired like most other K disciples, or he goes full Bobby Knight and ends up doing five to seven years in Rikers for an all-out brawl with some poor PAC-12 official in a meaningless game against Stanford.

Jeff Capel

After getting fired as head coach of Oklahoma in 2011 following two losing seasons and a cloud of NCAA investigations, Jeff Capel slunk back to Durham to become an assistant under Coach K. Apparently, it takes exactly seven years for athletic directors across the country to forget what a horrible head coach you were, because

Pittsburgh hired Capel as its top man in March 2018. While the four years after that were only slightly better than Kevin Stalling's 0-18 conference record at Pitt in 2017-18, Capel failed to break the .500 mark overall. Pittsburgh didn't finish higher than 11th in the ACC and topped out at a not-so-impressive conference record of 6-14 in 2021-22.

Don't sell that house in Durham just yet, Jeff.

CHAPTER 10

GRAYSON ALLEN PART I

Back in 2011 when we finished writing "Duke Sucks," we felt pretty good about the top 11 most hated Dookies of all time list we included in the book. Yes, we knew other guys would come along that we would dislike immensely and who would cause us to yell terrible things at our televisions – often in front of our families. But with most players staying only a year or two in college nowadays, truly hateable Blue Devils were a thing of the past. No one would ever be worse than Laettner, we reasoned. Surely JJ Redick's position was secure. No one was ever going to have a more punchable face than Wojo, we assured ourselves.

Or so we thought.

Enter Grayson James Allen.

When the first book hit store shelves, Grayson was but a sophomore at Providence School in his hometown of Jacksonville, Florida. Two years later, he would win the dunk contest at the McDonald's All-American Game, before entering Duke and embarking on a college and pro career that left in its wake a tsunami of dirty plays, bad sportsmanship, unprovoked trips, hip checks and indefinite suspensions.

For whatever talent Grayson had on the basketball court, his true aptitude seemed to be how he vaulted up the list of worst Dookies, crashing into the top 10 and leapfrogging to No. 2 in the personal rankings that we keep securely stored in our heads like an annoying song lyric.

If you're anyone but a Duke homer, this guy is public enemy number one. Just the mere mention of his name causes any self-respecting fan's aorta to seize with anger.

It's hard to overstate how much we personally do not like this guy. We'd never ever wish injury on a player, but he came about as close as we'll get.

But here's the thing. One-dimensional villains are boring. Darth Vader is intriguing because of his tragic backstory. Norman Bates isn't just a killer, he's a man fatally hung up by mommy issues. Hannibal Lecter is an erudite psychiatrist…who just happens to eat people.

The best villains are the ones who don't know they're villains.

We do a lot of research writing these books. We try to dig into the past and truly understand the players, the coaches, the history and why it all sucks so badly.

And you know what? Are you sitting down? The more we learned about Grayson Allen's past, the more we started rethinking the hate just a little bit. Or at least the more we struggled to put it in context. In a court of law, you might call what we learned mitigating circumstances.

Do they excuse all the crap that Grayson has pulled in college and beyond? Not a chance. We still really, really don't like him. But we leave it up to you to decide if his villainy is so straightforward.

Here's his story:

Grayson was the only biological child of Sherry and William Allen. They lived in Jacksonville, Florida, and when Grayson was eight years old, he came home from Grace Lutheran School telling his mom about a new kid in class that always smiled.

That kid – as it turned out – would have been excused if he hardly ever smiled. Tonan Ferrell had been given up for adoption by his mother when he was just eight, and he and his older brother were set to move in with their 18-year-old sister.

Grayson's mother had heard about the family and wanted to help. Tonan started coming over to the Allen house, and after a while, the arrangement became permanent. Grayson, an only child, had found a brother and a best friend. They shared a set of bunk beds, played video games together, and challenged each other on the basketball court.

It's a pretty good story, and don't tell us "The Blind Side"-ishness of it all doesn't make you think a little bit differently about Sir Trips A Lot.

The question is, if he was a good guy growing up and came from a seemingly caring family, what happened to him?

Allen apparently always had a temper on the court. He took losing hard. But he never had a rep for being particularly dirty in high school, 247sports recruiting analyst Rob Harrington told us.

"That question came up a lot once it started in college," he said. "I wouldn't have even described him as a fiery competitor, just sort of a regular, good high school player. There were guys over the years you could see issues brewing, like with [former Duke forward] Lee Melchionni. But Allen wasn't like that."

If there was a red flag in Allen's childhood, it's that he always wanted to go to Duke.

"He just admired the program immensely and viewed it as a good cultural fit for his style of play. The coaching staff identified him early, and that was a wrap," Harrington said.

Allen was always a bit of a brawler. He would go through five or six jerseys during a high school summer because opponents were always grabbing him and tearing his gear, Sports Illustrated reported.

During an AAU tournament in Richmond, Duke's then-assistant Jeff Capel watched as Allen took a blow from a defender as he tried to cut through the lane. A few minutes later, Allen retaliated with a stiff forearm of his own.

"He didn't take any crap from anyone," Capel told SI.

Around that time, Grayson was playing on the same travel team as future UNC point guard Joel Berry II. The two were friends. And even though their college choices would put them on opposite sides of the bitter rivalry, Berry seemed to have nothing but love for Allen. He called him a "great guy." If you're a Carolina fan, how do you square those types of comments with what we think we know about Allen?

So the question again is, where did it all go wrong?

Allen was the No. 24 recruit in the 2014 class – one spot ahead of his buddy, Berry – and was part of a murderous freshman class at Duke that included No. 1 Jahlil Okafor, No. 7 Tyus Jones and No. 13 Justise Winslow. With so much fresh talent joining an upperclassman core, the only thing Grayson had the opportunity to kick, punch or trip at the start of the year was the end of the bench.

And then Semi Ojeleye bolted for SMU in the dark of the December night and Rasheed Sulaimon was booted from the team.

The Tripper moved into the rotation.

As it turned out, he'd been learning behind the scenes how to get on the floor. He had ratcheted up the aggression.

"He would piss everybody off," Blue Devils then-assistant Jon Scheyer told Sports Illustrated. "You could ask Justise. Justise would always get into a thing with Grayson and want to fight him."

His teammates took to calling him "Deebo," the bully from the movie "Friday."

During April's national championship game, Grayson was a surprise contributor to the win and seemed on his way to a solid, if unmemorable, career.

Going into the 2015-16 season, fresh off of a championship and fueled by yet another top recruiting class, Duke was ranked fifth preseason. Grayson had moved into the starting lineup.

In the Devils' opener against lowly Siena, He Who Trips With The Leg led the team with 26 points. A star was seemingly being born.

And then it happened.

February 8, 2016. Duke versus Louisville in Cameron. The Trip Heard Round the World. At that moment, Allen's ongoing transformation was laid bare, a turn to the dark side suggested. But more on that later.

The question again is – what happened? How could Grayson Allen, an introvert who hated to be noticed and was so shy that his teammates had to drag him out to socialize, go from a solid high school player to a budding leader of a defending college champ to ultimately an unhinged, leg-flailing ankle sniper?

We're left with only one answer. Blame Duke. Or more specifically, blame Coach K.

Basketball programs are a lot like the military. It's probably one of the reasons Krzyzewski was so successful. He graduated from West Point and served in the Army. His mentor, Bob Knight, was known as "The General." K has said his time in the military influenced his coaching "immensely."

And the military works by completely breaking down recruits before rebuilding them again. A soldier's individuality is destroyed, his humanity sanded, so that he's able to do things he wasn't previously capable of – often horrible things.

The goal is to make the individual willing to take any action and sacrifice everything, in service of the institution. And in the process, he will earn the promise of becoming part of something bigger than himself.

"Today, you are Marines. You're part of a brotherhood," barked drill instructor Gunnery Sergeant Hartman, who was in charge of indoctrinating new recruits in 1987's "Full Metal Jacket." "Remember this: Marines die. That's what we're here for. But the Marine Corps lives forever and that means you live forever."

Replace "Marines" with "Duke," and you see where we're going with this.

Krzyzewski's motivating style also seemed to be lifted straight from boot camp. Some coaches get the most out of their players through X's and O's, kindness or encouragement. K drove them by serving as a tough-love surrogate father that the players were desperate to please – very much like that drill sergeant played by Lee Ermey.

"Because I am hard, you will not like me!" Ermey's character shouted in the film. "But the more you hate me, the more you will learn! I am hard, but I am fair!"

Krzyzewski was famous for making his players cry. He kicked them out of their own locker room, piling their belongings into trash bags. He broke clipboards and harangued them mercilessly. He once told his players during a game huddle, "Your f---ing faces suck!" Before another game, he showed the squad Mel Gibson's "Braveheart," then proceeded to run into the locker room brandishing his old Army sword, before plunging it into a flower pot.

If an organization is set up right, the institutional pressure it exerts can be incredibly powerful. It can change people – or at the very least amplify parts of their personality that were once hidden. Military training certainly has that ability, according to studies.

In "Full Metal Jacket," Private Joker goes from a wisecracking newbie to a hardened killer. Is that shift really that much different from what happens to some Duke players – especially those who stay for multiple years and have time to be indoctrinated by the system?

Could this explain why Christian Laettner put a footprint on Aminu Timberlake's chest? Is this why Gerald Henderson was willing to break Tyler Hansbrough's nose with just 17.5 seconds left in a

UNC-Duke game that was basically over? And is this why Grayson leaned into whatever tendencies he had for dirty plays?

It's just our theory. But you gotta admit, it makes sense, especially if Dear Leader is sending signals that he doesn't exactly disapprove of all this behavior. Laettner was left in the game after "The Stomp," and K called Henderson "the real victim" after that nasty elbow.

Let's remember one more line from our favorite cinematic drill sergeant: "It is your killer instinct which must be harnessed if you expect to survive in combat...It is a hard heart that kills. If your killer instincts are not clean and strong, you will hesitate at the moment of truth."

Krzyzewski has always been known for coaching right to the edge – and sometimes going beyond it. We think K recognized a certain churlishness in young Grayson early on, and he liked it. The coach even took to calling him "asshole" in practice.

And once the coach decided to weaponize those aggressive tendencies, there was no turning back.

CHAPTER 11

GRAYSON ALLEN PART II

By his second year, Allen was quickly transforming into the prototypical Dookie villain that we thought we'd never see again. He checked all the classic boxes. He was unlikeable on a molecular level, had an annoying smirk, celebrated small on-court successes obnoxiously and even slapped the floor on defense, like those Duke losers of yore.

But then, somehow, he got worse. Much, much worse.

Back to that 2016 Louisville game.

The No. 13 Louisville Cardinals arrived in Cameron to battle an unranked Duke squad that had taken a recent slide in the polls after several conference losses. The atmosphere was chippy even before the tipoff. The Cameron Crazies came out hot, determined to drag the Cardinals for their recently announced self-imposed postseason suspension.

The game was close much of the way.

With just under 14 minutes left in the second half, Duke was up 44 to 36. Allen drove to the basket and hoisted a double-clutch layup that missed everything. Allen fell to the floor. Louisville's Raymond Spalding snatched the rebound and turned to ignite a fast break up the court. He took one dribble and a frustrated Allen – still lying on the court – blatantly stuck out his foot, tangled up Spalding's legs and sent the Louisville player crashing to the floor.

The whistle blew, and Allen popped up, throwing out his hands as if to say, "Who, me?"

The Duke side looked incredulous, but there was absolutely no doubt Allen knew exactly what he was doing. "It looked intentional to me," former Dookie Jay Bilas said during the telecast.

Of course, it was intentional. A Duke booster could watch that replay 1,000 times and have trouble coming up with even the flimsiest of cases that it wasn't. Allen simply got frustrated and lashed out. Why hustle back on defense after you miss a shot when you can try to injure the guy that got the rebound and act stunned when he happens to bump into your leg?

After a review, the refs slapped Allen with a flagrant 1 but didn't eject him.

No punishment seemed forthcoming from Duke either. And maybe one of the reasons that K never did anything after this initial incident was that the dirty play seemed to spark something in the team and helped get the season back on track.

Unranked Duke ended up beating No. 13 Louisville that day, and after the game, the Leader of Men remarked on the team's apparent transformation.

"A couple of weeks ago, there is no way," Krzyzewski said. "I think we lose that game by 15 points because we wouldn't be able to get there."

Duke's Matt Jones praised the team's newfound "toughness," and we'll leave it to you to figure out what that might be code for.

The Blue Devils followed up that Louisville victory with a win over No. 7 Virginia and another over No. 5 UNC to propel them back into the top 25.

But the Cardinals would have their revenge. Just 12 days after their previous meeting, Duke and Louisville faced off again, this time at the KFC Yum! Center (still the dumbest name for an arena in all of college ball).

Louisville eked out a seven-point victory, but the real story was the message that the opposition seemed dead set on sending Allen. A little street justice was meted out. During one chaotic scramble for the ball, Louisville's Jaylen Johnson rocked Allen with an elbow to the face and then had to be restrained by the referee. In another sequence, Donovan Mitchell stripped Allen, pulled him to the ground, then slyly slapped him across the face.

It was pretty clear what was going on. Tough physical plays happen all the time at that level, but Allen's conduct during the previous game was out of bounds – he'd broken the code – and Louisville was out to correct his behavior in the same way prison inmates do with a child molester.

But if Allen learned his lesson, he had a funny way of showing it.

Florida State came to Cameron a few days later. As the game's final seconds wound down with Duke up by 15, the Blue Devils committed a turnover. Xavier Rathan-Mayes, who had been guarding Allen off the ball, turned to join a potential fast break, but Allen stretched out his left foot, catching the FSU player's leg and causing him to tumble. No foul was called.

After the game, Grayson wasn't exactly contrite. "He wanted to keep playing physical, so I tried to walk away from it as he was grabbing me," Allen said after the game. "We ended up tangling up and falling. It was really nothing."

Er, we guess? Though if you watch the replay, it's pretty clear that's not at all what went down. This was clearly an intentional act, and the second time Allen had done an opponent dirty in a single month. College basketball fans, the media – even "SportsCenter" – were beginning to notice. There was no denying it anymore: The tripping was becoming a Thing, it was becoming a pattern.

Certainly, now was the time to correct course, to bring the hammer down, right?

Right?

Of course not. The ACC – in perhaps the vaguest punishment yet invented by man – announced it had issued the Duke player an official "reprimand." Oh, no! A reprimand. That's one step above a furrowed brow and just below a stern letter of concern.

What does a reprimand mean, you ask? As it turns out, absolutely nothing. It's sort of like when the Academy Awards punished Will Smith for slapping Chris Rock by handing him a Best Actor Oscar.

Coach K, on the other hand, took seriously the embarrassment of having one of his players publicly called out by the league, and he vowed to do everything in his considerable power to make sure it never happened again.

Nah, we're joking again. He did none of that. The coach said he'd handle the matter "internally" and responded to the ACC's reprimand with a dose of whataboutism.

"What [Allen] got was the stiffest reprimand a player has gotten in our conference this year," Krzyzewski said at the time. "There have been other guys who hit people and whatever and no reprimand. I'm not knocking our conference. I'm just saying I thought they took action. And then you have to move on."

And if Allen had moved on, It's possible we might have forgotten about the whole thing. Except Allen didn't move on. And it was becoming clearer by the moment why he didn't. If you don't correct a child when he poops in the sink, don't be surprised when you find poop in your sink.

Early the next season, No. 5 Duke met Elon – Elon! – in one of those meaningless pre-conference tune-ups where the opposition is just there to collect the TV revenue.

With about four minutes left in the first half and Duke up by eight, Elon guard Steve Santa Ana drove the baseline against Allen, and just as he was spinning back to his right for what was going to be an open shot, Allen's right foot shot out and hooked Santa Ana's knee, sending the Elon playing spilling to the ground. A technical foul was whistled on Allen.

Grayson reluctantly made his way to the bench and proceeded to have one of the most epic meltdowns in the history of college basketball. He screamed, "This is bullshit!" as K tried to calm him down. He punched a chair before Jon Scheyer stepped in to keep him from punching something – or someone – else. After more head shaking and reddening of the face, Allen finally shoved a towel into his face.

The Duke star finished the game with 3 points on 1-8 shooting. Just another display of the maniac that Grayson had become.

Or so we thought.

Again, context doesn't excuse actions. But it might help explain them.

Something we didn't know: Two days before that Elon game, a young woman named Savannah Goodman died at Duke Hospital after a life-long battle with a severely compromised immune system. She, like Allen, was from Jacksonville and had matriculated to Duke at the same time. Allen had read her story and started visiting her. The two became friends.

So, maybe it wasn't just being called for a tech that set Grayson off that night? Was he actually struggling with some other, more personal issues at that moment?

The story of their relationship made it into The Florida Times-Union after Allen's mother called columnist Mark Woods to get

Goodman's contact information. Is it possible that she planted the story to land her son a little positive publicity at a time when he was becoming college basketball's primo villain? It's possible. It's also possible that Allen made the visits for the same reason.

But in the end, we have no idea. It's equally possible that Allen was a legitimately good person from a legitimately good family who – for some reason – was spiraling before our eyes. You can see our struggle in trying to write about him.

Nevertheless, you'd have to think that the third tripping incident in a calendar year would be the tipping point. To quote James Bond author Ian Fleming, "Once is happenstance. Twice is coincidence. Three times is enemy action."

At this point, someone would surely have to do something. Duke and Coach K could no longer hide. Even the usually Duke-friendly media was starting to ask questions. Dick Vitale – the most slobbering partisan of Duke partisans – consulted his bald dome index and ruled against the Duke star. "Can't understand the behavior of…Grayson Allen @theACC has no choice but must discipline / Enough Already," he tweeted, no doubt with a fat tear streaming down his cheek.

Once you've lost Dookie V, that's pretty much curtains. The day after the game, Duke finally caved and announced it was suspending Grayson "indefinitely," as well as stripping him of his team captaincy.

Finally some justice, we thought. But then we began to wonder, what exactly does "indefinitely" mean? Dan Patrick, on his radio show that week, asked the same question of Coach K.

"Well, it means it gives me time as a teacher to teach," the coach said, the smarm dripping out of the speakers. "There's not a ten commandments of tripping…Each situation is different."

Patrick pushed back, asking how Allen could explain this happening three times.

"Someone doesn't make mistakes three times? How does anything happen, Dan?" K fired back angrily.

Krzyzewski said during that interview that the suspension could be three games, it could be two weeks. He just didn't know.

As it turned out, "indefinite" meant one game. One. Measly. Game.

Allen sat out Duke's next contest, a conference-opening loss to Virginia Tech, and the Leader of Men had seen enough. Grayson was back the very next game against Georgia Tech. And not only was he back, but he was also back in the starting lineup. That oughta learn him.

Krzyzewski was apparently so touchy about any criticism of Allen that he froze out ESPN commentator Jay Bilas – one of his former players – blaming Bilas for everything bad the network had to say about Grayson. When Bilas later came to Durham to call a Duke game, he walked onto the court and K "literally turned his back on him," according to ESPN The Magazine.

"I think it's appropriate, and I think the things that we've done are appropriate," Krzyzewski said of Allen's punishment. "There are things that you see or the public see, and there are things that you all don't see and shouldn't see or shouldn't be talked about, and they're called teachings. You don't need to teach out in the public all the time."

Would you be shocked to learn these "teachings" didn't stick?

A few weeks after the Elon incident, Allen was at it again – this time forcibly shoving an FSU assistant coach out of the way as he tried to save a ball near the Seminoles' bench. A couple of weeks after that, he nearly caused a bench-clearing brawl when he committed a cheap frustration foul on Wake Forest's Bryant Crawford. Tempers flared, the two players jawed at each other, Duke's players stood up off the bench and Wake's Brandon Childress was given a tech for rushing to his teammate's aid.

Then there was what sure looked like an attempt to trip Virginia's Kyle Guy off a screen, and a kick to Virginia Tech guard Justin Robinson while going for a loose ball. And on and on and on.

Now fast forward to an ACC Tournament semifinal against UNC, on March 9, 2018. In the last minute of the first half, Carolina was up by three. Allen put up a floater while clearly trying to draw a foul. None was called. UNC grabbed the board and was off to the races the other way. As Carolina forward Garrison Brooks ran past Allen, the Duke player thrust his butt into the sprinting Brooks, knocking him to the floor. He was tagged with yet another flagrant foul.

Anyone else see a pattern developing here? Grayson gets pissed that something doesn't go his way – be it a missed shot, a bad defensive play or the failure of the refs to call a phantom foul – and instead of hustling back on defense, he decides it'd just be easier to lay out one of his opponents.

That game was a fitting (almost) end to Grayson's career at Duke. You couldn't have scripted it more perfectly: losing to UNC, getting a flagrant foul on a cheap play and his coach doing absolutely nothing to try to correct the behavior.

"Do you think that was the only time someone was hipped in the game?" Coach K snapped to reporters after the game. "If you look in the low post, it's going on all the time. So it happened at half-court. They got it. It's done. And that didn't win or lose the game."

If this were a movie script, we'd call this the climax – the point where the action is resolved and the story moves toward its conclusion. Only this is not a happy ending.

Earlier intervention might have made a difference, a different path might have been possible. But now it was too late. This was the moment when that black helmet slid down atop Anakin Skywalker's head, or when Joker from "Full Metal Jacket" executed a young enemy sniper. Allen's fate was sealed.

CHAPTER 12

GRAYSON ALLEN PART III

Grayson Allen left Duke in 2018 as arguably one of the most hated college athletes of all time.

And that's not just us saying that. It's also Sports Illustrated, USA Today, countless blogs, YouTube videos and someone's grandma on Reddit.

The thing is he could have changed all that in the NBA. He could have rehabilitated his rep. The League could have provided a fresh start. Allen would be under less pressure, would enjoy a lower profile and he'd be free from the Gothic Duke hellhole and its tough-love drill sergeant, whom Allen seemingly would go to any length to please.

Leave the tripping behind, young man, and scrape out a professional basketball career!

It wasn't very long after Grayson was chosen 21st by the Utah Jazz that it became pretty clear that rehab just wasn't going to happen. A mere two months after draft night, Grayson was up to his old tricks again.

During a 2018 summer league game – we repeat, summer league – Allen got into a scuffle with Atlanta Hawks rookie star Trae Young.

Allen fouled Young hard as the Hawks guard was going up for a shot, clamping Young's arm. As the two players untangled themselves, Grayson gave Young a shoulder bump to the gut for good measure. The officials quickly moved in, and Allen threw his hands into the air in his usual, "What, me?" pose.

He hadn't even played in a single real game, and he was already stirring stuff up.

If you had any hope for Allen's redemption, at this moment it pretty much evaporated like a puddle of Gatorade on Cameron's floor. What the hell was Grayson doing?

The human need to belong is a powerful thing. We have a fundamental desire to feel like we're accepted and valued. So what happens when you're Grayson Allen and you've spent a good chunk of your adult life having it made absolutely clear to you on a daily basis that every single person – outside of a few Duke fans and your teammates – absolutely hates your guts?

That's psychologically unsustainable. A human being is not built to be the villain his whole life.

When he first arrived at Duke, Grayson admitted that the booing crowds bothered him. As a high school star, he hadn't encountered that kind of reaction before, and he wasn't quite sure how to handle it. Fair enough. It had to be overwhelming to be 19 years old and have an entire arena of 20,000-plus raining down abuse on you.

Teammates could help, creating a bubble that a hated player can safely live inside, making it easier for someone like Allen to convince himself that it wasn't about him.

That's just what Allen's teammates did at Duke. They made sure to change the channel when something negative came on about Grayson or helped him laugh off the negative press. They reassured him that he was not the bad guy. This was just about Duke haters, they told him. They'd always been that way.

"I don't feel like it's just on me now," Allen told The Fayetteville Observer in 2016 during his sophomore year. "I know that my teammates have my back. We've kind of taken the mindset that we're taking the boos as a team. It's on all of us, we're not singling out one player. I know that they all have my back, we're together as a team."

OK, easy enough. But then, what happens when the boos keep clobbering you day after day, season after season? Your brain starts to crack as it tries to reconcile the cognitive dissonance between the good person you think you are and the total asshole the rest of the world is painting you as.

To preserve your mental health, you basically have two choices. You can admit that the haters are right, that your behavior has been out of bounds and commit to sincerely making a change. Or you can embrace the hate, and wear it like a badge of honor.

Guess which path Grayson chose?

Other Duke players have done exactly the same thing. Guys like JJ Redick and Christian Laettner used negativity as motivation.

"It's surprising to me if I didn't get booed as I walked out onto the court," Allen told The Washington Post in 2018 as a senior. "I've kind of just accepted it. I feed off of it. I'm not only used to it, but I own it now."

Owning it is a lot easier than coming to terms with the legitimate reasons tens of thousands of strangers around the world hate your freakin' guts. But we get the shortcut.

By his NBA years, being a jerk became part of his brand. It was part of his identity. Some people were into poker or painting as a hobby. Grayson's was being a complete bastard. Without that, what was left? He would just be a second-tier professional player who was abnormally hated.

So he apparently decided to just lean into the jackassery.

In his second year in the NBA, he found a way to get ejected from a summer league game, which is kind of like getting kicked out of your elementary kid's trivia night for cheating. And Allen's team was down 23 in the fourth quarter when it happened.

Allen, then playing for the Grizzlies, shoved the Celtics' Grant Williams to the ground and was slapped with a flagrant 1. The very next play, he took a swing at Williams' head.

"Just get him out of this game now," disgusted commentator Dan Dakich spat.

The referees agreed. Mr. Bad Sport was tossed. And just like every time before when one of these things happened, Allen threw up his hands as if to say, "Oh, wow, how did such an unfortunate thing ever come to pass?"

That was hardly the end of his early NBA misadventures. The hits kept coming. In a 2020 regular season matchup, Grayson went after Trae Young again, appearing to try to trip the Hawks star while chasing him around a screen.

Young later posted a clip of the incident on Twitter, writing, "Damn... tell me what y'all see!! Smh this gotta stop.! #ifyoudontknownowyouknow"

Allen shot back on the app, "Damn that must've really really hurt. I'm sorry. I hope you're okay."

But his worst incident was yet to come.

January 2022. Fiserv Forum. Bulls guard Alex Caruso drove the lane on a breakaway and went up to lay in the ball. Allen – now playing for Bucks – wrapped his arms around Caruso in mid-air and flung him violently to the ground.

Allen was tossed. As he left the court, he could be seen smirking.

"Grayson Allen giggling after receiving a flagrant 2 and being ejected seems pretty on brand for him," Richard Jefferson wrote on Twitter.

After the game, Caruso was not amused. "Dude just kind of grabbed me out of the air. It was kind of bullshit," he said.

Allen provided his usual deflection. "It was very unfortunate how it played out. I jumped to block it with my left and as I'm spinning, went to grab the ball with my right hand not throw him down," Grayson said. "It was a really hard fall, and I'm glad he's OK. If I could do the play over again, knowing he'd fall like that, I wouldn't make the play."

Tests later revealed that Caruso had broken his wrist. He had to sit out eight weeks to recover. Allen was suspended for – you guessed it! – a single game. Seemed fair.

The incident was definitely one of the dirtier plays in recent NBA memory.

"Kick Grayson Allen out of the NBA. I don't care," tweeted Bulls blogger Jason Patt.

The Chicago Sun-Times called Grayson a "punk," a "sneaky, dirty weasel" and a "clear and present danger."

"Grayson Allen is damn lucky he's not playing the Bulls of my youth when Norm Van Lier and/or Jerry Sloan would have been there to bring the retribution," ESPN's Michael Wilbon wrote.

The Bulls of old might have been gone, but the Bulls of new still took Grayson's antics personally. Shades of Louisville. When the

Bucks arrived to play Chicago a few months after the incident, Bulls center Tristan Thompson did not hold back.

"Take one of my dogs out like that, we're gonna have issues," Thompson said before the game. "What [Allen] did affected one of our guys, and I don't think anyone should forget about that…I think guys have [it] in the back of their head. And if guys wanna play chippy, let's play chippy. I like it. I like a little blood and sweat."

Dirty Grayson was booed without mercy during that game (and many others). When asked about it later, he replied flippantly, "That was weak. I've had way worse in college."

Yeah, probably from your former coach.

Allen was consistently treated so disrespectfully by opposing fans that his own team started booing him. It just seemed to be the thing you did to Allen. That face of his was practically begging for it. The Bucks started booing him in practice as a joke, but when they discovered it motivated him, they started doing it during games.

"They have so much fun doing it. I think it's funny," Allen said at the time. "I think it's honestly hilarious that they've kind of turned it into a fun thing. It makes hearing it out there during the game a lot easier too, because they think it's so funny."

Whatever gets you through the night, my dude. We can't help but think back to teenage Grayson, the kid whose family took in an eight-year-old boy and whom Joel Berry said was "a great guy." How far Allen had fallen.

In April 2022, a data analysis company called Sidelines.io crunched more than 10,000 social media posts about NBA players to see which one was the most hated.

You probably don't need us to tell you what happened next.

Allen won, and it wasn't even close. He beat the second-place finisher by a mile and was also the only player on the long list – the only one – with more negative overall online reactions than positive.

This is what happens when someone's worst impulses get weaponized, when unsportsmanlike behavior is never properly punished, when someone surrounds himself with people who continually condone his bullcrap and help him mentally hide from it.

And it all started at Duke.

"Mike has been an esteemed professor…at Duke for some 41 years. Wherein his curriculum has been constructed around endless life lessons and service," Duke's athletic director Kevin White said at Krzyzewski's 2021 retirement press conference.

Question is, what were those lessons?

CHAPTER 13

THE DUKE MUSEUM

A few years ago, Duke had an idea…another it seemingly borrowed from UNC. Why not start a museum dedicated to the basketball program? The so-called Crazies Wall opened in 2018 and is meant to be an immersive, tactile experience. Fans are allowed to touch all the objects embedded within, including jerseys, balls and pieces of the courts the Devils slapped on the way to two of their championships.

We think it's incomplete though. For a true Duke experience, we've got five more objects the school should consider adding.

Marker
Plastic resin, polyester, oily silicone polymer
Mike Krzyzewski, 2014

Coach K tossed this marker in disgust after the officials dared to call a foul on Andre Dawkins. The writing implement bounced off the floor and hit then-assistant Steve Wojciechowski in the leg. K received a technical foul.

Nike PG 2.5 shoe
Leather, fabric, foam, rubber
Zion Williamson, 2019

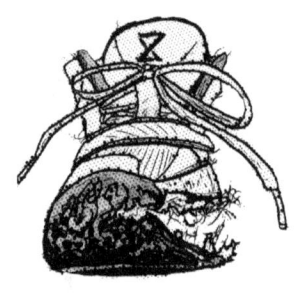

Williamson tore this shoe in half during the first minute of a game against UNC. The malfunction reportedly caused Nike's stock to tumble 1.05% and shone a spotlight on the sometimes gross relationship universities like Duke have with shoe companies.

Letter to The Chronicle
Newsprint
Tom Large, 2020

This letter appeared in the student newspaper. It was harshly critical of the Duke basketball fans – and was curiously written by an alumnus. The writer shared his horror in discovering students weren't actually filling Cameron and that he'd been able to buy a ticket in the student section for an ACC game. "Last night I witnessed with embarrassment a 'TV-side' student section that was empty from the baseline extended!" he wrote. "For a home conference game vs. Miami (who has beat us five times in recent years) on ESPN. Unbelievable…Y'all need to step up your game."

Diamond Pendant
Black diamonds, gold
Rafaello & Company, 2009

This pendant in the shape of Jesus' head was one of five jewelry items Duke forward Lance Thomas purchased from an exclusive New York City store. The total cost was $97,800. Thomas was then a senior in college. Historians remain unclear on where he got the money.

Condom
Latex, foil
Cameron Crazies, 1984

This condom was thrown at Maryland player Herman Veal during a game at Cameron. A year earlier, Veal had been accused of making improper advances on a female student. (The university later cleared him.) The Crazies decided to throw objects at him, including women's undergarments. The vulgarity caused the university's then-president to write a letter to the students demanding they shape up.

CHAPTER 14

THE GROSSEST RETIREMENT TOUR

The biggest display of vanity in college basketball history began on a humid June day back in 2021. Coach K dropped the needle on Cascada's "Everytime We Touch," spit on his comb, parted his hair perfectly down the side for the three billionth time, pulled on a terrible Duke-blue suit, and took the stage at Cameron Indoor in front of adoring university bigwigs, journalists and fans.

And so commenced a year-long farewell tour that was remarkable, not just for its hubris, but for how it ended in a fashion so epically tragic that even the most seasoned Duke haters couldn't have dared imagine it.

But before we get to how it crashed and burned, we have to go back even farther – back to fall 2020. The presidential election was raging, COVID rode the breeze and Duke began a shortened season ranked in the top 10. The Devils returned a solid core of Matthew Hurt and Wendell Moore, as well as three other top-25 recruits and looked formidable.

It wasn't long though before the season began to feel...different. The team eked out a 10-point win at home against Coppin State and lost to Michigan State.

It was fast becoming clear that this Duke team just didn't have it. Maybe chalk it up to the hangover of wasting three top-ten picks the last time there was a tournament. Whatever it was, they just weren't that good.

K clearly sensed it too, and sure seemed to be looking for a ripcord.

Back in September before the season tipped off, Krzyzewski threw out the idea that every single eligible Division I team should be allowed into the postseason tournament.

"An all-inclusive postseason tournament will allow a unique and unprecedented opportunity for every team and every student-athlete to compete for a national championship," the coach said in a statement, like a freshman high on shrooms for the first time and just riffing on the universe.

Somehow, some way, the NCAA tournament had to go on, the coach said, because the organization couldn't afford to cancel its marquee event again as it had the previous season.

By December 2020 and a few poor performances later, K had done a complete 180. After a bad loss to Illinois, Krzyzewski suggested that maaaybe the whole season should be canceled. "I don't think it feels right to anybody," he said, before going on to bristle at the suggestion that he was just saying that because he'd gotten his "butt beat by a lot."

The season wasn't called off. And Duke didn't improve. The squad fell to Virginia Tech early in 2021, and the L ejected them from the AP polls for the rest of the season.

The team finished 9-9 in the conference and a pitiful 13-11 overall. And on Selection Sunday, Duke's name was not called for the first time since Coach K's "back injury" forced him off the bench back in 1995.

Without Duke playing in March, the whispers started – as they always did when a blue-blood program stumbled or when a coach who had patrolled the sidelines for so long suddenly wasn't performing as well. Was Duke's time over? Had the game passed Krzyzewski by? Would the fans get impatient and turn against the program?

Those whispers never got any louder because K had the perfect solution. A few weeks later, he threw his little press conference and announced his retirement a whole damn year early.

Officially, Krzyzewski was giving his two weeks' (plus 50) notice for the benefit of his players. "It's not fair to a kid that you would be recruiting," the coach said at the time. "Like, yeah, I think I'm going to coach and then, at the end of the year, say you're not coaching."

Dragging out your goodbye for an entire season was the "only thing, really, you could do," Coach K assured us.

Right, unless you consider what nearly every single other great coach had done. John Wooden announced he was retiring just before his final game. Dean Smith: after the season. Roy Williams: after the season. Jay Wright: after the season.

But Coach K was different, and there was absolutely no way he was going to ride off quietly into the sunset, like those other names had.

Throughout his career, Krzyzewski had always paid lip service about doing what was best for his players – you know, "the kids." It was the right thing to say publicly. But it probably wasn't long into his coaching career that he realized "the kids" would come and go, but there was only one piece of crucial connective tissue between seasons – beyond Duke's royal blue Pantone 287 U/C – and that was him. He was not some aw-shucks guy caretaking a storied program for a couple of years. He *was* Duke basketball.

And for Duke basketball to be served, he had to be served.

The coach who made everything all about himself for his entire time at Duke wasn't going to miss out on a victory lap in which the sports world could collectively feed him grapes and rub oil on his craggy feet.

For anyone except the most loyal Duke fans, K's retirement announcement was bittersweet. On the one hand, he was finally going. We'd finally, finally be rid of him. No more watching his constipated face on the sidelines, no more hearing his nasally whine during press conferences, no more having to sit through endless Dick

Vitale hosannas during a game, no more of his stupid commercials choking the channels during March.

But on the other hand, Duke haters knew that the price for him going was high. So very, very high. We were going to be forced to stomach the most epic, the grossest, the most prolonged, insufferable and embarrassing slobber fest ever witnessed on the planet Earth. All you could do was pull on your Kevlar underpants and brace yourself.

And it turned out to be just as bad as we all feared. And worse.

Every game was a coronation, a genuflect from coaches, fans, media members and the guy selling popcorn in section 212 – just as Krzyzewski knew it would be. As it was required to be.

You doubt that? Never forget, when Duke visited Chapel Hill in February 2022 for Krzyzewski's last game at the Dean Dome, the Tar Heels chose to simply acknowledge the rival coach's retirement before tipoff as opposed to launching a full-scale Mardis Gras. Some inside the Duke program "bristled" at the proper lack of respect, according to ESPN.

Other opponents fell in line much better.

During halftime at the Champions Classic, the event's other coaches – John Calipari, Tom Izzo and Bill Self – gushed over His K-ness during a Madison Square Garden jumbotron video that CBS noted "seemed to go on forever."

In February, Syracuse gave Krzyzewski a plaque made from a piece of the old Carrier Dome's roof and created a scholarship in his name. In March, Pittsburgh produced a tribute video and gifted him a sculpture of an iron fist.

It also wasn't hard to see that K retiring was one of the greatest gifts the sports media had ever received. The only thing that would top it would be Tom Brady unretiring yet again at age 60 to join the

UFC. With K, suddenly the college basketball season had a compelling storyline ripe for the flogging. Every Duke game suddenly had much more meaning, whether it was against Gardner-Webb or North Carolina. Eyeballs and ratings were absolutely guaranteed.

And every broadcast of a game was preceded by breathless fawning and punctuated with graphics like, "K's final ride." The producers slapped together wistful packages with lots of slow-mo, lamenting, "This could be the last time Coach K eats an ice cream at the John Paul Jones Arena." The game introductions always included K not-so-sheepishly soaking in a standing ovation. This went on the whole damn season. You couldn't escape it. It was awful.

"Look, I didn't stay this year to have a farewell tour. I stayed because I wanted to coach one more year," Krzyzewski said after a February game against Boston College, in which his opponent honored him before tipoff. "When a school takes some time out and says 'We recognize that you've been pretty good for the ACC and for basketball,' that means a lot."

Do us a favor. Put down this book. Turn off your phone. Lock yourself away in a dark closet for a few seconds. Take a deep breath. Quiet the noise in your head. Ignore everything you may have heard and ask yourself, do you honestly think Krzyzewski didn't set up a farewell tour so he could collect all those accolades? Do you honestly believe he thought he deserved anything less? That he hadn't calculated that announcing his retirement after the season, when casual fans weren't paying as much attention to the sport, would have meant he wouldn't have gotten months of wall-to-wall coverage and would have done a disservice to his greatness and legacy?

What does your brain tell you?

We know what our brains are telling us, and we agree with former UNC great Tyler Hansbrough. He compared the Duke coach's farewell tour to that episode of "Curb Your Enthusiasm" in which Albert Brooks threw his own funeral while he was still alive so he could hear all the nice things his friends would say about him.

"I thought it was one of those situations," Hansbrough said. "I thought it was funny."

And one more thing: Krzyzewski was arguably the most powerful person in all of college basketball. If he truly didn't want any of those nauseating tributes, he wouldn't have gotten them.

But no matter what was happening during pregame ceremonies and on ESPN, for K to earn the biggest honor, Duke still had to put it together on the court. No one would say it within the Duke program, of course, but this season was different. It was bigger. The team suddenly had a massive amount of pressure thrown on it to send Coach K out on a high note – maybe the highest note possible. K wanted that storybook ending, the players wanted it, the media wanted it and the history books wanted it.

The Blue Devils looked built to do it (which, again, we're sure never crossed K's mind when he chose this season to retire). Heralded freshmen Paolo Banchero, AJ Griffin and Trevor Keels joined big man Mark Williams and seasoned junior (is that a typo?) Wendell Moore to form another potentially lethal squad.

Things looked good early. Duke dispatched Kentucky in the opener and a few weeks later beat top-ranked Gonzaga.

The squad hit a few bumps as the season dragged on, losing to Ohio State and Miami. But as the regular season drew to a close, the Blue Devils had reeled off seven wins in a row and had risen to No. 4 in the polls. They looked scary. They looked unstoppable. All that was left was to send UNC packing in Krzyzewski's final game at Cameron, then run the table in March.

The dream of K riding off into the sunset with a championship seemed all but certain. The script was written.

That is until it wasn't.

North Carolina came into that final regular season game reeling. The team had fallen out of the top 25 months before, and the team's play had been inconsistent all season long. Duke had slapped their arch-rivals by 20 one month earlier in Chapel Hill, and everyone expected Duke to do it again at Cameron.

The hype was tremendous. ESPN planned to cover the event with what they termed a "megacast." The network decamped to Durham three days early and offered live, onsite reports during halftimes of men's college games. Other plans included live reporting all Saturday long starting at 7 am, a special two-hour "College GameDay" and during the game itself, a Krzyzewski cam that stayed glued to the coach for all 40 minutes. Following the game, the network would broadcast a tribute to the coach from the Cameron floor.

The atmosphere inside Cameron was like a Final-Four-meets-the-Super-Bowl. One Duke fan paid $1 million for four tickets. Jerry Seinfeld and NBA commissioner Adam Silver were in the stands. The university invited all 208 of Krzyzewski's former players, and nearly 100 of them were set to attend. The players were all given white pullovers with the "One K" logo on the breast. Notably, Christian Laettner and Wojo were the only players who didn't wear them during the game. Laettner likely opted out because he was the only person in the room with an ego bigger than K's. Wojo probably hawked his on eBay to make up for that sudden lack of a Marquette paycheck.

Before the game, K's former players gathered on the court and formed two lines, creating an arm tunnel that the coach could walk through on his way to center court – a move we haven't seen since a peewee soccer game. A photographer then snapped a group photo from the rafters, where another banner would no doubt be hanging soon. (Hilariously, the TV audience saw none of this because the previous game on ESPN happened to go into overtime. Hubris, meet karma.)

The national anthem played, K stifled tears then gathered his team for one final Cameron pregame huddle, after which he dabbed his eyes with a tissue.

All the pieces were in place. The outcome was foregone. The last few pages of the story just had to be transcribed. Duke had thought about every single detail on this momentous day.

Well, except one: their opponent.

The game began with Duke tipping the ball out of bounds. On North Carolina's first possession, Caleb Love drove the baseline and flicked a pass to a cutting Armando Bacot for a thunderous dunk. It was like a body shot that rocked every single smug person sitting in Cameron and an announcement that maybe this wasn't going to be so easy after all.

North Carolina played from behind most of the first half but remained in striking distance. The team had toughened considerably since the soft showing in Chapel Hill a month before.

In the second half, UNC tied it up early but then quickly fell behind again by seven. The team clawed back though, keeping the same five players in without a single substitution.

Bacot tossed in a turnaround layout with 9:21 left and UNC took the lead – a feat that the announcers noted seemed "impossible" based on the first game and much of the first half.

The crowd stayed in it, screaming their usual cheer sheet nonsense and resting assured that Duke would find a way, as they always had in the past.

With just under two minutes left, Leaky Black tipped in a layup to put the Tar Heels up eight, Paolo Banchero missed on the other end, and you could feel the air begin to leak out of Cameron Indoor like a slow fart out of grandpa. The boisterous cheers that had filled the arena all night turned to concerned murmurs.

On the ensuing possession, Love drove the lane, dished to Bacot and thrust out his tongue as the center threw down yet another slam.

For the Dookies, the play was like receiving an uppercut from an 18-wheeler – a shock so harsh, it nearly broke reality. At that moment, they were forced to accept what seemed inconceivable for much of the game and for the days they had spent camping out in the cold to gain access. Duke was going to lose. Carolina was going to have the audacity to beat Coach K in his final home game.

As the clock ticked down, several fans started crying. The former Duke players rubbed their faces and stared off into space, wondering how the hell this happened. Christian Laettner, wearing a baseball cap and a graying goatee, gazed up at the scoreboard with a puzzled look like a kindergartner trying to understand quantum physics. Coach K appeared angry and annoyed – like he always did.

Final score: UNC 94, Duke 81.

As the reality of what had just happened sunk in, a sort of "what now?" fell over Cameron. The crowd looked paralyzed. Should we stay, the Cameron Crazies probably wondered, or should we go back to the dorms and start drowning our sorrows in a sixer of White Claw? They had absolutely no idea what to do, how to react because they – like everyone else involved, from the university, to the cable network, to those fans in the Bert and Ernie costumes – never for one single second had planned for the chance that real life would deviate from the prepared script. (Paolo Banchero admitted in December 2022 that the game had indeed been all about Coach K. "We didn't even really practice or, like, game plan that week," he said.)

"All that rah rah for what?" Love tweeted shortly after the buzzer. "What they gone say now?!" Bacot added.

It was a good question. But the show had to go on. And several minutes after the horrific loss, a scrum of Duke dignitaries appeared for the carefully choreographed ceremony marking the final game. K, red-faced, appeared, and with the determination of a murderous robot, snatched the mic, walked to center court and proceeded to go off script using a voice usually reserved for scolding young children after they've colored on your Porsche.

"Everyone be quiet!" he snapped. He then called the loss "unacceptable," a characterization we couldn't help but notice that threw his team under the big, steel-belted radials of a giant motor vehicle and backed over them a few times. He ended his embarrassing tantrum with a ray of hope – and a promise. "The season isn't over, all right?"

True enough.

Carolina had spoiled the party that night. The team had come into K's house and humiliated him and his team in front of celebrities, former players, fat-cat alumni who'd paid thousands for the privilege of being there and 3.98 million viewers on TV. Duke's student newspaper said it felt like the "end of the world for Duke men's basketball."

But it was not the end.

Duke fell short in the conference tournament a week later, but no matter. March Madness loomed. K still had one more shot at redemption, another chance for his story to be written in the way that he and every single person in the media had hoped.

As potentially one of the top seeds, the Blue Devils were asked by the NCAA in which region they'd like to play. Duke reportedly chose Chicago, Krzyzewski's hometown. It was a location that would provide the emotional bookend the coach was clearly hoping for and generate four billion more gauzy TV packages scored with soft piano plinking. (Duke ultimately ended up a No. 2 in the West.)

The Blue Devils opened the tourney by dispatching Cal State Fullerton and Michigan State, then outlasted a scrappy Texas Tech team. As the clock ticked down in those last two wins, Krzyzewski turned to his bench and his family sitting behind it and pumped his fist, as if to say, "The ride continues!" – but also, "We didn't go out like suckers as we had so many years before."

Moving into the Elite 8, the media began truly salivating.

"They are 40 minutes away from a fairytale Final Four, rising to a moment that was foreseeable in theory months ago but now is taking on tangible form," Sports Illustrated wrote.

Of course, you know what happened next. Plumes of sulfur gas living on Venus probably know what happened next. Duke downed Arkansas and North Carolina destroyed St. Peter's, setting up the first tournament face-off for the rivals.

It was bound to happen one day. Most fans – both UNC and Duke alike – probably just hoped that the day would be approximately eighty years after they were dead.

The match-up was arguably among the most anticipated and hyped in March Madness history, its import made ten trillion times greater by the fact that Krzyzewski was in his "final ride," as ESPN had reminded us every 30 seconds since November. The Guardian suggested the game might be the "biggest in college basketball history." The Ringer touted it as the "matchup of the millennium."

We have no idea what Coach K was thinking in the moments before the Final Four game against UNC tipped off. Was he just happy to be there, satisfied that his team had pulled him this far, given him a respectable showing, and anything else from here on out would be gravy?

Or – and this is what we believe – he was terrified, knowing full well that there was more on the line over the next 40 minutes than pretty much any game he'd ever been a part of. It wasn't just about moving on to the championship or keeping his vainglorious retirement tour alive for another two days. It was about going through a rival in a historic game to do it. And losing would have eternal consequences – we mean, like, literally eternal. Your most hated rival would gain bragging rights over you for decades, if not forever, and your legacy – already crapped on a month earlier at Cameron – would be partially defined by how and to whom you went out. Had, say, Kansas or Villanova sent Krzyzewski packing in his final game, few would likely remember. It would be a trivia question. But to lose like this risked staining his record like bacon grease on a shirt. It was never coming off.

The actual game was everything viewers had hoped for. The teams battled each other every single second on the floor, making one incredible play after another. Banchero looked deserving of being a top NBA pick. Bacot pushed through on a bum ankle. Brady Manek tossed in threes like he was casually pitching wads of paper into a wastebasket.

With 1:18 remaining, the lead had changed hands 17 times. Duke led by one, 74-73. Coach K's wife left her seat to make her way down to the court for the presumed coronation.

But then, Carolina jumped ahead by a point, Mark Williams choked away two free throws and you could just feel the universe winding up for perhaps the most classic ending in a rivalry littered with them.

Seconds later, Caleb Love brought the ball upcourt, paused just over half-court and casually dribbled as he watched the action unfold. Black raced over to set a screen, Love moved to the top of the key then fired what was about to be the second-greatest shot in the history of Carolina basketball (after Michael Jordan's game-winner, of course). His three put North Carolina up four and jammed Duke into a coffin.

In the remaining seconds, as Carolina sealed the game with free throws, Coach K could only sit on the sidelines, his face sourpuss, watching it all slip away. There went the game, his shot at another title and his chance to earn one more game's worth of residuals from his AT&T commercial.

There's a piece of advice often given to trial lawyers: Never ask a question you don't know the answer to. Something similar goes for retirement tours. There's probably a reason most coaches don't opt to take a season-long victory lap, even if their egos were that big. The unknown is not your friend. All the planning, all the hype and media coverage and all the wishing won't make a bit of difference. The sport is going to send you out how it's going to send you out. It could be with a storybook ending. Or it could be with two absolutely crushing losses to your most bitter rival that will likely be remembered long after your record is forgotten.

Coach K News Roundup

In his final years before retiring in 2022, Coach K didn't slow down one bit. Even in his mid-70s, he still miraculously found the energy to continue being the cantankerous piece of beef jerky he'd always been. Inspiring.

In case you missed them, here are a few of our favorite post-2012 stories.

You Can't Spell Jerk Without K

One of the first public glimpses of Coach K's true nature came back in 1990 when he summoned ten student-newspaper reporters to his moist Cameron lair and dropped a profane and scatological tongue-lashing on them for daring to award his team a B+ grade.

The encounter revealed the highly-paid coach to be petty, thin-skinned and arrogant.

In the decades that followed, those around Krzyzewski claimed that he had mellowed with age. But if anything, he seemed to get more entitled. Check this out:

During a January 2022 game against Georgia Tech, Michael Devoe – then the ACC's leading scorer — talked some good-natured trash to K and the Duke bench. Instead of doing what any first-year high school coach would have had the discipline to do and ignoring it, Krzyzewski completely lost his cool. He called a timeout, stormed out of the coaching box and proceeded to chase Devoe up the floor. "You don't know who you're talking to," Devoe said K barked, sounding less like an esteemed athletics coach and more like a C-list celebrity trying to get a table at Nobu. K then turned his whining toward the refs, chewing their ears as the blood pooled in his ever-reddening face.

Still, he wasn't done. After the game, K first lectured Devoe in the handshake line, then admonished his coach, Josh Pastner, proving that Krzyzewski could have coached for 1,000 more years and still would have been the same amount of condescending jerkwad.

Something similar happened back in 2016. Late in Oregon's 82-68 win over the Blue Devils, Dillon Brooks hit a three as the shot clock wound down, then celebrated by throwing up three fingers. After the game, Krzyzewski homed in on Brooks like a guided missile to give him a dressing down.

"You're too good a player to be showing off in the end," Brooks said K told him.

But when asked at the postgame press conference if he had indeed said that, The Leader of Men, The Teller of Truth, The Teacher Who Happens to Coach Basketball, denied it.

"I didn't say that," Krzyzewski snapped. "You can say whatever you want. Dillon Brooks is a hell of a player. I said, 'You're a terrific player.' And you can take whatever he said and then go with it, all right?"

Dude was straight-up lying. Audio of his exchange with Brooks mysteriously leaked online (must have been a Carolina or

Kentucky fan in the TV truck that night), proving that K had said exactly what Brooks had claimed. The coach was forced to issue an apology – though it came out as more of a classic non-apology that chalked his lie up to reacting "incorrectly" to a reporter's question.

And one last one – an incident that takes us full circle to where this all began. It was January 2021. Duke was in the midst of a disappointing year, having lost four of their first nine contests. Then came another L at Louisville, dropping the Blue Devils to .500.

At the postgame press conference, a Duke student reporter asked Coach K an innocuous question about what the team's "next step forward" would be.

Instead of just, like, answering, Coach K decided to hike up his pants, grab a ladder, climb up on his high horse and proceeded to belittle the reporter in the most excruciatingly arrogant way.

"Why don't we just evaluate this game?" the coach said, using the same tone that we imagine Mariah Carey might have deployed after discovering the wrong brand of bottled water backstage. "I'm not into what our next step forward is right now. We just finished a hard-fought game."

Then K turned to the classic intimidation tactic that was a favorite of dictators and Hollywood assholes everywhere: throwing a snotty question back at the questioner.

"What's your major? What's your major at Duke? What's your hardest class?" the coach demanded.

The reporter answered economics, and K fired back, "OK, say you just had the toughest econ test in the world, and when you walked out, somebody asked you, 'What's your next step?' You see what I mean? Do you have some empathy? Just give us time to evaluate this game and we'll figure it out, just like we always try to do."

Only they didn't. Duke missed the tourney that year for the first time since 1995.

Family Ties

Just imagine for a second that you're married. And imagine the somewhat fraught relationship that many husbands inevitably have with their wife's father, with all of that "you stole my little girl" energy.

Now imagine that father-in-law is Mike Krzyzewski. Kinda gives you chills, doesn't it?

Having to spend Thanksgiving with the steely, smile-free former military jagoff is enough to make you pack up your stuff, call a divorce lawyer and trek thousands of miles to Mount Doom to toss in your wedding ring. Can't you just picture Coach K screaming red-faced at you for the wrong choice of pie?

And sure enough, marrying into his family turned out to be as much fun as you might have expected.

Apparently K, being K, was constantly in search of petty mind games to wield and power plays to deploy in order to assert his dominance. He also apparently fancied himself a gardener.

So when his daughter and son-in-law moved into a house that had a tree out front that the elder Krzyzewski didn't like, the coach made sure to lecture the couple every time he visited.

K's advice: "You need to send a strong message, plant-wise, when people come up to your home," the son-in-law told The Washington Post. "And that's just a sad-looking tree."

The couple refused to remove it. We mean, obviously. Who goes to someone else's house and starts lobbing design criticism before they've even walked through the door?

And if you thought K would just let the whole tree thing go and allow someone to make a decision that defied him – even if that decision involved their own damn front yard – you've probably never watched a single one of his games.

The coach continued to pick at that scab nearly every time he saw his daughter and husband. He offered to replace the tree or threatened to drive over under the cover of darkness, back up his luxury Escalade and rip the tree out of the yard.

The son-in-law told him if he did that he'd sue or call the cops. He was joking. Sort of.

A Big Blue Asterisk

Krzyzewski became the all-time winningest college basketball coach in February 2019. You might have seen a news story or two about it. Or watched as the angels descended from heaven to anoint his head with boot black.

The moment was disgusting for so many reasons – one of the biggest being that The Rat had to pass some true legends of the game, including Dean Smith, to slither onto his perch.

But maybe the worst part was how the moment once again revealed the disgusting, horrible, no-good, head-bangingly frustrating double standard that exists with all things Duke basketball.

You could make a pretty strong case that K was actually a few dozen wins short of the record, had he been treated like every other coach in the NCAA. It's not like Duke and its beloved headmaster hadn't been touched by serious scandal over the decades. And some of those scandals have been pretty open-and-shut. Let's just revisit one, as a for instance.

Remember Corey Maggette? Played for Duke during – you guessed it – a single season back in '98-'99. He was later ruled ineligible to suit up because the NCAA discovered he'd accepted payments in high school from AAU coach Myron Piggie (best name ever).

Piggie was sentenced to more than three years in prison. Another player he'd paid, UCLA's JaRon Rush was given a lengthy suspension and his school was forced to forfeit $45k in revenue.

But Duke? Nothing. Nada. That statue of the three monkeys covering their eyes, ears and mouth. The school – officially, at least – was allowed to skate because the NCAA determined that Duke didn't know Maggette was ineligible. And what's more, they decided Maggette didn't know either. (So he forgot he took the payments?)

Plenty of other schools have been through similar cases over the years, including Michigan, which had wins vacated in the 1990s for payment to players.

Even Krzyzewski's good buddy Jim Boeheim – who was chasing him on the wins list – had 101 Ws wiped from his record because of ineligible players.

Then there was the curious case of Duke's Lance Thomas, who somehow managed to buy $100k worth of jewelry from a high-end Manhattan store while still in college (as one does). The NCAA definitely wasn't going to let that stand. The governing body rolled up its sleeves, threw on its deerstalker cap and launched a hardcore investigation.

And you know where that one went.

Thomas refused to speak to them, and the case was closed, clearing Duke of any wrongdoing based on the evidence the NCAA had dug up…which was none.

The stakes couldn't have been higher. Thomas had been a member of the 2010 national championship team, and the Blue Devils could have had that banner thrown in the trash like Memphis did with Derrick Rose.

But no. Krzyzewski and Duke walked away scot-free yet again. Rules for thee and not for me.

So if you ask us, K isn't the all-time winningest. We'll never think of him that way, no matter what the record books or what his wife may try to tell people while cornering them in the parking lot of a Durham Kroger.

So congratulations, Coach Boeheim. We always did like Syracuse.

Krzyzewski's Kommercials

It started back in 2005 with a get-me-a-bucket AmEx ad in which Coach K – shot in an extreme close-up fit for a Sarah McLachlan charity spot – declared, "I look at myself as a leader who happens to coach basketball."

Having that guy's face beamed into living rooms forty times a day was unsettling enough for viewers, but it was especially alarming for those in collegiate athletics. They worried the commercials gave Duke a recruiting advantage over other schools whose head coach hadn't sold out to hawk revolving debt. The NCAA president at the time received several phone calls from athletic directors and conference commissioners expressing their extreme displeasure.

But if the man himself had any moral qualms about appearing in Kommercials, he got over them pretty quickly. Back in 1997, Krzyzewski hired David Falk – the super agent behind Michael Jordan – to boost his earnings off the court. In the years to follow, K reportedly looked at endorsements as a way to make up for the money he missed out on by not jumping to the NBA, according to the Triangle Business Journal.

In the seasons leading up to his retirement, it was damn near impossible to watch a college basketball game in March without seeing his pinched face come on screen right after a Buffalo Wild Wings commercial. He appeared in spots for GM, Allstate, Capital One and AT&T.

That last commercial debuted in his final year, 2022, and like his previous efforts, featured a performance so wooden you would think his father was Geppetto.

Remember the spot? He appeared with the brand's mascot Lily – or sort of appeared. The commercial had a weird uncanny valley feel, as it sure looked like the two actors were shot in different locations and the film cut together, probably owing to Krzyzewski's schedule. Or maybe Lily was sponsored by Adidas.

The premise of the ad is that the coach is applying for a job managing an AT&T store.

"I'm really confident I'd be successful at it," K deadpans to Lily because ha ha, retail is only for dummies and requires no experience or expertise or skill, and a monkey – or someone who's done literally any other job – could do it. We wish someone at K's last press conference had asked him what his strategy would be to increase individual transaction size and to optimize inventory control in his AT&T store.

Whether his ads were good or bad, the question we were always left with was, why even cast him in the first place? He's not likable, he's not funny. He's also divisive. Half the country already hates him – and the other half was going to as soon as they saw him try to deliver a scripted line.

The reason brands use him is probably the same reason they have always used well-known people in their ads. They want to transfer some of the celebrity's value and special magic to their product.

But what stinks is that these commercials aren't really using Coach K – they're trading on the myth of Coach K, a carefully crafted image that has been built over the decades by the media, PR hacks and a wealthy private university.

We're still waiting for a commercial that uses the true Coach K. Maybe he could cut a spot for a movie theater where he scowls and orders a crowd to "quiet down!" AMC, get in touch with David Falk.

11 Things UNC Fans Will Never Stop Talking About From The Last Game at Cameron and the Final Four Game

For UNC fans, the stretch from March 5, 2022, to April 2, 2022, will go down as one of the greatest in the rivalry. It's hard to imagine two more rewarding wins in what has been a hard-fought, back and forth series. Besides the wins themselves though, Heels fans will never let go of a laundry list of specific, amazing moments. Here are just a few of our favorites. And if you're a Kentucky fan or a Maryland fan or just a pure Duke hater, we realize some of these things might be petty, silly or inconsequential. Just sit back and bask in it. We'd appreciate it.

- The TV cameras cutting to a desperate Jay Williams in the stands signaling for a timeout after UNC went on a run during Coach K's last game at Cameron. Too bad, Jay. Nothing was stopping the train that night.

- "Unacceptable." K had planned a huge party for the Cameron postgame, and when he still had to come out and address the crowd after taking the L, that's how he described the game. Oh, no, Michael. It was quite acceptable.

- "Bang bang, motherfucker!" What Brady Manek shouted after draining yet another three in Paolo Banchero's eye during the Final Four. This phrase should be etched on the facade of the Smith Center.

- Duke assistant Chris Carrawell blowing off Hubert Davis in the handshake line after the Cameron game. Stay classy, Chris.

- The groaning sounds the Cameron Crazies made every time Brady Manek got an open shot. We want to make this noise our ringtone.

- The Crazies crying through their blue makeup and Sesame Street costumes during the postgame. It's always delicious when Duke loses at home, but the tears, cheap blue makeup and pure incredulity of March 5, 2022, made it even tastier.

- The white pullovers given out to all of the former Duke players, of which we're pretty sure 99% were thrown in a closet never to be worn again. (You just know that Lee Melchionni will wear that thing to every Rotary Club function in the hopes that someone, anyone will remember that he played at Duke.)

- Mark Williams grimacing after missing two free throws with 44 seconds remaining in the Final Four. He could probably feel K's icy glare burning into the back of his skull.

- Cascada, which Duke used as their hype song during the team's Final Four intro video.

- Mickie Krzyzewski walking along the sidelines before the game ended to either A) be ready to celebrate with her beloved K in the tunnel, or B) getting the heck out of there to not suffer the loss.

- The thought that people paid hundreds of thousands of dollars to get into Cameron on March 5. And celebrities like Jerry Seinfeld, Adam Silver, Kyler Murray, Dirk Nowitzki and Terrell Owens thought it would be that important to be seen during such an event. Only they all left with a big, fat L.

IS THE UNC-DUKE RIVALRY DEAD?

When UNC guard Caleb Love dribbled to the left of the key and drilled a three over the outstretched hand of Devils center Mark Williams, he sealed the last and final L in Coach K's career, sending

The Rat scurrying into retirement. In the Final Four. At the hands of his bitter rival.

The two teams finally clashing in the NCAA tournament was a moment that casual college basketball fans – and TV executives – have been slobbering over for decades. But had you asked nearly any Heel or Blue Devils fan, you'd have gotten a very different answer. No way in hell they'd ever want to see that happen. And for good reason. Losing during the regular season was bad enough, but losing during March Madness would be a trump card that the winner could hold over the loser's head forever and ever.

And after Love and the Heels snatched Duke's soul that night, fans and observers were quick to dump several thousand truckloads of dirt on the UNC-versus-Duke grave.

"The rivalry is over," USA Today wrote. "UNC has won. Duke came in second. Nothing can happen in this series from this point forward for the Tar Heels to relinquish the lead."

Maybe so – flexed bicep emoji – but was that night truly the end of the rivalry?

For the 40 years that marked K's reign of terror, Duke basketball has been associated with success, sure, but it had also largely been intertwined with the Kult of Personality that was Michael Krzyzewski. His shadow loomed over Jon Scheyer's transition and will loom over all future coaches. (It pretty much had to. K, ever the generous humanitarian, never gave up his Cameron office. He forced Scheyer to set up shop one floor below.)

But the burning question that every rivalry fan has had to confront is, what is Duke without Coach K? We mean besides 1% more likable and a bit less profane?

With so many players leaving early or jumping into the transfer portal, coaches became the only constants in college basketball. It's fun to hate Duke, but if they turn into Wake Forest or Boston College (other small private colleges that are mostly non-factors in college basketball), the sports world will have become a worse place.

The UNC-Duke rivalry during the K era had its ebbs and flows. In the beginning, K was the new Kid on the block, trying to take on the exalted Dean Smith. When K first stalked the sidelines in 1980, UNC was only a few years removed from a tough loss to Marquette in the 1977 championship game – a Tar Heels team that was considered the best in the country.

One season after K arrived, a freshman named Michael Jordan hit one of the most memorable shots in college basketball history to beat Georgetown and earn Smith his first national title. Carolina dominated those early years against its instate rival, winning eight of the first nine meetings and 12 of the first 16 through the 1986-87 season. During that stretch though, K started to build a solid team, including a squad that made it all the way to the 1986 title game before losing to Louisville.

From the moment Christian Laettner arrived on campus in 1988, the tide began turning dark blue. Starting with a three-game sweep, Duke won eight of the next 14 and capped off K's second straight natty in 1992, crushing Michigan by 20 points in the final. Duke fans across New Jersey sat back in their lounge chairs made from the skin of the undeserving and smirked at the fact that Dean Smith and North Carolina were now in their rearview mirror. Duke and K had taken the mantle as the Kings of college basketball.

A mere 12 months later, Chris Webber called a timeout he didn't have, and UNC came right back with a championship of their own, Dean's second. Duke lost in the championship the very next year.

The point is, the rivalry always went in waves, and there have been several times when one side was sure that it was D-E-A-D, dead.

Carolina ripped off seven wins in a row in the mid-90s. K bolted for "back surgery." The rivalry felt over.

Duke won 15 of 17 during the transition from Bill Guthridge to Matt Doherty to Roy Williams. That included another championship loss in 1999, K's third title in 2001 and a Final Four run in 2004. Dean was gone, Doherty was awful. Over and done. Put a fork in it.

Then Carolina won seven of the next nine, which included the season of Roy William's first championship in 2005 and his second in 2009.

Seven months later in November of 2009, the top recruit in the country, Harrison Barnes, picked UNC over Duke. If you weren't there at that moment, you can't appreciate how much that seemed like the final nail in the coffin. While Barnes wouldn't suit up for another year, Roy Williams was stacking talent at Carolina like firewood before a Yukon winter. "You had your run, Duke," UNC fans were thinking, "but Roy came home from Kansas, and now UNC will take it from here, thank you very much."

Tar Heel fans – us included – were too busy dancing on the Blue Devils' Gothic grave to notice what happened next. Hubris and overconfidence in this rivalry have a way of stepping up and smacking the offenders squarely in the face.

The very next year, K rode a team of upperclassmen to a victory over Butler and captured his fourth championship – the same number as Roy and Dean combined. Then Carolina fell off the face of the earth after most of their 2009 roster graduated or left for the NBA, and in 2010 the team missed the NCAA tournament for the first time since the forgettable Doherty era. K loaded up on one-and-dones and slithered into Indianapolis to win yet another national championship in 2015.

K was King. Carolina was mired in an NCAA scandal. Roy soon missed on recruit after recruit. Pack it up. It was over again.

From that moment, Duke and UNC split their next 16 games – during which Carolina took home the 2017 crown – before K's final humiliation at Cameron.

But Devils fans were no doubt certain that redemption and their next "the rivalry is over" moment was going to come with K walking off the court for the final time with his sixth national championship. Fortunately, we all know what happened next.

Back and forth. Peaks and valleys. Duke versus UNC is a windy mountain road with no visibility as to what's ahead, other than the knowledge that it will be thrilling.

It's important to understand the crazy swings that have always been part of the rivalry and to avoid recency bias.

We heard all the chatter after that 2022 Final Four win that it was over, and honestly, a part of us wanted to believe it. There would have been nothing better than never having to think or worry about Duke and their special band of floor-slapping, fist-pumping losers ever again.

But we gotta be honest: It wasn't over then, and it will probably never be over. It's more like a new chapter has begun. Or more likely, a whole new book.

It's true though, when we lie in our beds at night, stare up at the ceiling and send our minds zooming to the farthest reaches of the universe, we can't imagine what could possibly top UNC beating the coach that made Duke Duke in his final game. In the Final Four.

But what we have learned from spending an unhealthy amount of time researching, thinking and writing about Duke and this rivalry is that it's like horror-movie villains or boy bands. Cannot be killed. Somehow, someway, just when you think the final sentence has been written, it's time to pick up the pen again.

Truthfully, we don't want it to be over. Yes, that final win over K was glorious – as good as any pleasure available on this earth that doesn't involve a Bojangles chicken sandwich. That win, and the emotional release that went with it, is unlikely to ever be replicated. But we want another chance for something that magical to happen again. Even if it means suffering through another Austin Rivers shot. Even if it means enduring another smug Christian Laettner copycat. Even if it means the media salivating all over itself about how perfect Duke is.

Sports rivalries give a lot of people meaning, and it's all within a somewhat safe space. We need the escape of getting indescribably jubilant or irate over the way some 20-year-old kid bounces a ball. It's stupid really. But it's also kinda awesome. And we need it. As much as we hate to admit it, we don't really want Duke to fall off the map and become just another team.

You need darkness to discern light. You have to experience evil to appreciate the good. We may have needed a guy like K, with all of the awfulness, to truly enjoy an irrationally confident Caleb Love hitting the dagger of all daggers. Otherwise, it might have been just another shot.

Statistically Speaking - Who Won the Rivalry during the K era?

UNC and Duke played exactly 100 times during K's time at Duke and the record finished a perfect 50-50. Duke fans will tell you that K held a 50-48 edge because Pete Gaudet fell on the sword for two of those losses but, screw that. He is taking those Ls. Clearly, the win at Cameron in K's final game and the Final Four win to send K into retirement were enormous, but how do we weigh them to figure out who truly came out on top during those 42 years? We're talking just head-to-head matchups and not overall accomplishments during this time (total ACC regular season wins, total championships, etc.). We looked at several factors that felt like situations where a win was worth a little more: road wins, upsets (defined as when there is a ranking difference of greater than 10 and the underdog wins), upsets when one team is ranked No. 1, ACC Tournament matchups and, of course, the NCAA Tournament. And we swear on the grave of Rameses II that we created the scoring system before we analyzed the games. No gaming the system here, like never playing a true road game to pump up your early-season record. This, in our minds, is the final word. Let's go.

ROAD WINS (worth one rivalry point each)

UNC won 20 times at Cameron Indoor.

Duke won once at Carmichael and 17 times at the Dean Smith Center.

EDGE: UNC by two.

UPSETS (worth one rivalry point)

UNC won 10 times as a major underdog.

Duke won four.

EDGE: UNC by 6.

UPSETS OF No. 1 TEAM (worth an extra rivalry point)

UNC beat Duke five times when the Blue Devils were ranked No. 1.

Duke beat UNC just once when the Tar Heels were No. 1.

EDGE: UNC by four.

ACC TOURNAMENT MATCHUPS

(UNC fans should look away now, this is ugly)

Of the 14 times these two met in the ACC Tournament, Duke won 10 times to UNC's four. That includes one Duke win in the quarterfinals, a four to one advantage for Duke in the semifinals and a five to three advantage in championship games. EDGE: Duke. We give them one rivalry point for the quarterfinal win, two for each semifinal win and three for each championship victory. That's a total of 13. Ouch.

NCAA TOURNAMENT MATCHUPS

For K's final game at Cameron, we've already given UNC the points for the road win and the upset so it's worth at least another rivalry point. That evens the score at 13 with only the Final Four game to judge. Hmmm. How many points would that count for?

FINAL SCORE:

UNC - 1,000,013

Duke - 13

CHAPTER 16

THE BLANK PAGE PART II

When we wrote the first book, we thought it would be a fun joke to include a blank page in the book for readers to fill in any future Dookiness that occurred after the publication date. We never imagined that after 10-plus years, we would have enough material to fill an entire second book. We're again giving you a page to write whatever you like, but this time, it's more metaphorical. We know there will never be enough space to capture all the crap they will pull, so this blank page represents an infinite future where the suckitude of that place in Durham will live forever.

Thank you to...

Tate Frazier
Joel Tesch
Bryan Tucker
David Drake
Martin Murphy
Kevin Canevari
Rob Harrington
Haley, Zack, Tyler, Kayla, Pavel, Kelly and the rest of the gang at Bottle Theory

Visit DukeStillSucks.com for exclusive merchandise, including signed books and the opportunity to get a personalized essay written by the authors on the Duke topic or player of your choice.